COMING TO MOKENA
FINDING NEW FREEDOM

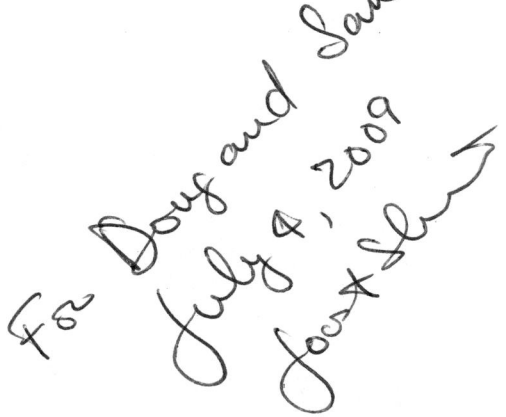

JOOST SLUIS

Outskirts Press, Inc.
Denver, Colorado

The opinions expressed in this manuscript are solely the opinions of the author and do not represent the opinions or thoughts of the publisher. The author represents and warrants that s/he either owns or has the legal right to publish all material in this book.

Coming to Mokena
Finding New Freedom
All Rights Reserved.
Copyright © 2009 Joost Sluis
V2.0

This book may not be reproduced, transmitted, or stored in whole or in part by any means, including graphic, electronic, or mechanical without the express written consent of the publisher except in the case of brief quotations embodied in critical articles and reviews.

Outskirts Press, Inc.
http://www.outskirtspress.com

ISBN: 978-1-4327-1139-9

Outskirts Press and the "OP" logo are trademarks belonging to Outskirts Press, Inc.

PRINTED IN THE UNITED STATES OF AMERICA

FOREWORD

Americans often hear talk about those who come to the United States to "escape oppression" with little understanding of what that means. After World War II many people came to the United States to build new lives. They came to find opportunity and freedom. Those who came rarely told their story.

The older highways of the United States are lined with homes that were hand built by their owners. Many were constructed by families recovering from World War II. Some were the families of veterans and others were new Americans from foreign lands. The homes were built without power tools and often took years to complete. They were often recognizable by being slightly out of proportion or of unusual design. The brave people who built them left them to us as monuments to their grit and courage.

This book is about a couple of rich young people from a small almost forgotten city in The Netherlands. Their story begins with a short history of the city and country they came from. Small countries like theirs that existed hundreds of years ago are now provinces or strange names on a map. The history of their ancient country is rich but largely forgotten.

Willem and Ann were accomplished people from West Friesland – a country of strong men and women. Their future was bright when they married in 1939 but war destroyed all their plans. We meet them and follow them throughout their lives.

As vassals of the German Third Reich during Word War II they and their children experienced debasement, violence and starvation. Ann hid her Willem and four neighbor men in the crawl space under her town house for eighteen months to save them from labor camps. When the war ended their fortune was gone and they were barely alive. They survived because of heroism, determination, and faith.

After the war they sought better opportunities in America. Their journey exposed them to a new culture and new trials. Because of the immense freedom they found in the United States they were able to start over and reestablish themselves in a small Illinois town. They built their own house, made a good life for their children and pursued their new American dreams. Their lives ended in triumph.

ACKNOWLEDGEMENTS

William and Ann Sluis talked often of the ordeals they had suffered in World War Two. Ann was fond of reminiscing about their lives before the outbreak of war and about her honeymoon on the Riviera. Simon J. Sluis, William's half brother, wrote a monumental history of the Sluis family that included a complete genealogy. Together with some additional historical research and fact checking, the recollections of William, Ann, Simon and the Sluis children are the basis for this book.

The author wishes to thank his brother William Sluis Jr. and friend George Griffiths for editorial help, encouragement and advice.

Mokena, Illinois
November 15, 2008

CHAPTER 1
ENKHUIZEN

The northern coast of Europe from the English Channel to Denmark is outlined by a long row of islands. Most are very low and some of them are used for farming with dikes surrounding them to ward off the North Sea while others have large sand dunes and are popular for tourism. Many centuries ago these islands were the Northern coast line of what are now The Netherlands and Germany. In the past two thousand years, the North Sea has greatly altered the land.

The land on this Northern coast is called Friesland. (Fries rhymes with trees) The Germans call their part East Friesland. The Dutch call their part the provinces of North Holland, Friesland and Groningen. It is a country of low lying farm land, dikes, windmills, and constant awareness of the power of the North Sea. A line of large forested sand dunes forms the shore line of the English Channel in the west.

Charlemagne ruled Friesland in the eighth century and converted the tribes to Christianity. The Vikings ruled in the ninth century and they in turn were driven out by the Germans in the tenth. Small towns appeared on the North Sea coast starting about the year 1000.

The Netherlands has the largest lake in Western Europe, the Ysel Lake. The lake occupies the center of the country with Amsterdam near its Southern end and smaller cities on the West and East coasts. A large modern closure dike forms the northern shore. The lake is fed by two main rivers, the former river "Y" from the west, now converted into canals, which drains the western swamps and the river "Ysel" from the east, which is a tributary of the Rhine. About half of the Ysel Lake was drained in the twentieth century to produce new land.

Two thousand years ago Pliny and Tacitus of Rome called Lake Ysel by the name Flevo. Flevo was a land locked lake surrounded by low lying islands, swamps and mud flats that drained into the North Sea through a river at its Northern end called the Vlie which was situated between the current Friesian islands of Vlieland and Terscheling.

High tides and huge storms on the North Sea during the eleventh and twelfth centuries washed away much of the land in Friesland. The northern coast was inundated to create a string of islands where the coast used to be. Large areas of land were flooded and the river Vlie disappeared into the sea. Lake Flevo was now a shallow salt water bay of the North Sea that became known as the Southern Sea or Zuider Zee. A peninsula that reached into the Zuider Zee from the West was called West Friesland. A small seaport on the new North Sea coast was founded at Medemblik.

Travel from place to place was mostly by boat. Many lakes and the river "Y" to the South isolated West Friesland from the rest of the world and the area developed its own language and customs. The land was very low and wet with large lakes and many areas that were barely dry enough for habitation. Life was short in the swamps, with regular epidemics of water borne and cattle diseases. Malaria was a common cause of death. Famine was frequent because of unpredictable weather. The people were tough and strong. The only road to the south ran over the sand dunes along the English Channel from Alkmaar to Haarlem. The Counts of Holland built defensive forts at Beverwyk to keep the northern savages from attacking Haarlem.

Leather and animal skin shoes have been worn for thousands of years but they rot in the swamps. Mud produces heavy clumps by sticking to most footwear. The inventor is long forgotten but the wooden shoe was a great improvement over animal skin footwear and was ideal for the frisians. The shoe is custom fitted to the wearer's foot and is made from beech wood. Beech wood has unusual properties since mud does not stick to it and it gives very sure non slip footing on wet boat decks. The wooden shoe was so much better than the much cheaper leather shoe that it became the standard. Wooden shoes became the symbol of the land and the people. The normal version was unpainted but beautiful decorations were painted onto those made for formal dress.

In the twelfth century, some monks were given a piece of swamp land South of West Friesland in an area then called Waterland. The monks knew the art of damming land and built an enclosure for their property that became a model for future progress. The town is Monnickendam, named after the dike the monks built. The art of the monks was later called "inpoldering" which means to surround low wet land or shallow water with dikes and pumping out the water to make dry land. An area of farm land made in this way is called a "polder". An extra strong dike for a city is called a "dam".

The first report of a sea dike constructed to protect West Friesland from the North Sea was made in 1250. All of West Friesland was ultimately surrounded by a protective dike. Dikes are stabilized by using large mats of reeds that are placed on the bottom and held in place with rock ballast, which is not available in the swamps. Stones were purchased in Germany.

Trade with inland Europe by boat, primarily on the Rhine River, was extensive. The West Frieslanders had developed a durable hard cheese that became a major trade commodity. The culture began to center on cattle.

This time was the beginning of what was later known as the "Little Ice Age". Giant North Sea storms continued to change the shape of land and sea. In 1334 storms made the harbor at Medemblik less accessible because of shifting sand bars. In 1346 the Black Death claimed thousands of the Frisians.

Enchusae had been given its first rights as a village by Count Jan I in 1299 and in 1355 it was incorporated with the nearby town of Gomerskerspel to form the City of Enchusae. The city named Enchusae in the West Frisian language would later be called Enkhuizen in the language of Holland. Count William V granted city rights and granted a coat of arms that showed three herrings with gold crowns on their heads.

Heavy storms in 1361 caused construction of a new larger and better protected Enkhuizen harbor inside the West Frisian dike. The new harbor made the city the main seaport on the Zuider Zee. The city competed with Hoorn, located a short distance south. Because the sea was shallow with an average depth at its Northern end of about twelve feet and at its Southern end of about three feet, Enkhuizen's location at the Northern entrance of the sea was the best. A weighing house was built in 1394 to support the trade in butter and cheese and a second harbor was built in 1400.

On the Feast of Saint Elizabeth, November 5, 1421 a large part of West Friesland was flooded by a huge storm that also flooded much of the other low lying provinces of present day Netherlands. Enkhuizen lost parts of the city and its church and later reconstructed its church inside the dike to build the Church of Saint Pancras – now the Zuider Kerk or Southern Church - that stands today. The farmers of Gommerskerspel built their church as the Church of Saint Gommarus - now the Wester Kerk or Western Church. Wars over fishing and commercial rights caused the city to build a new defensive wall that was completed in 1549.

The Calvinist movement of Christian reformation was a strong influence in West Friesland and all the Low Countries. The new Calvinistic religion had been suppressed by King Philip II of Spain who ruled Holland at that time. The resulting uprising produced the 1566 "Beeldenstorm" (image storm) where iconoclastic Calvinists stormed all the Catholic churches, removed all the priests, brothers and nuns and destroyed all the images inside and outside the churches in the belief that they were all idolatrous. Churches were painted white on the inside and renamed as old, new, south or west as a result.

The Calvinists religious police carefully searched all homes and buildings to ensure that no religious images were left in them. When this was done families were left with no practical way to teach Bible stories to their children. Images in the churches and homes had been mostly paintings and symbols representing various stories from the Bible that the illiterate Hollanders had used as teaching aids. The people soon found out that the tiles on the outside of their stoves and in fireplaces were exempt. In Holland and Friesland the manufacture of white tiles with Bible stories on them grew rapidly. The tiles became famous. Images of persons were also permitted and caused the development of the Dutch school of famous portrait artists while the rest of the painters in Europe were still painting religious art.

The Reformation created a major breach between the Calvinists and noblemen who supported freedom to choose a religion on the one hand and Philip II of Spain and his support of the Catholic Church on the other. Philip II believed it was his duty to support the Church. To crush the rebellion, he sent a new governor to the Netherlands, Ferdinand Alvarez de Toledo, Duke of Alva. The Duke imposed harsh rule on the people, had several counts decapitated, installed a new criminal code and sent garrisons of troops to the major cities, including Enkhuizen. Early in the morning of Ash

Wednesday 1568, fifteen hundred suspects of heresy were rounded up in the Low Countries and executed.

Orange is an ancient city state in southern France that was ruled by the Nassau family in the 1500's. In 1572, Prince William of Orange, with several ships of savage men, captured some small towns on the English Channel coast of Zeeland, south of Holland. Other small channel ports joined with William and provided money and encouragement in a spontaneous uprising against Spain. William then sailed to Enkhuizen which was controlled by Calvinist rebels. On May 21, 1572 the city joined William of Orange against Spain, calling itself the "Key to the Zuider Zee". The Spanish garrison was eliminated and the "Dutch Republic" was born. William of Orange converted to the Calvinist faith. The defenses of the city were strengthened further and the harbor defense fortress Willigenburg was built. The city gate of Willigenburg, the Drommedaris, (The dromedary because it supposedly looks like a one humped camel) remains to this day. In 1593 the city was further strengthened by a new city wall that included seven bastions to landward. Other harbors were dug at the same time.

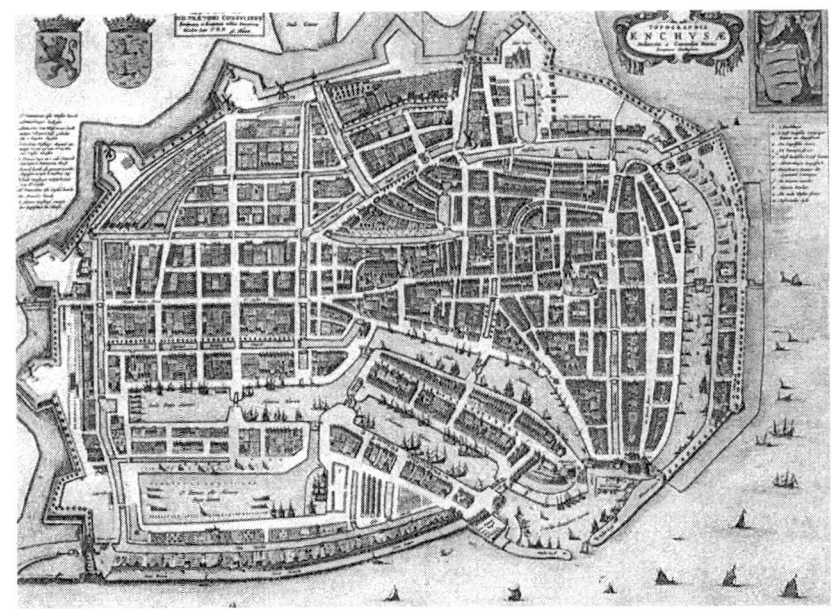

"Map of Enkhuizen in the 16th Century"

The war divided the Low Countries into Protestant and Catholic. Several peace conferences between the Northern areas of the Low Countries and the southern parts failed to bring peace. Extreme Calvinist violence in Ghent in 1578 caused three Southern provinces to form the "Union of Arras" to defend the Catholic faith and reconcile with Spain. A few weeks later, the provinces of West Friesland, Holland, Zeeland and Utrecht responded with the "Union of Utrecht" that banded them together to defend religious tolerance and independence from Spain. Ultimately seven provinces banded together as the "United Provinces" of Holland/West Friesland, Zeeland, Utrecht, Gelderland, Overyssel, Friesland and Groningen. Holland and West Friesland were both ruled by the Count of Holland and were treated as one entity. William of Orange was expected to lead the Seven Provinces but he was assassinated at Delft in 1584. The union then offered its crown of kingship to Henry III of France and to Elizabeth of England but both refused. Maurice of Nassau, son of William of Orange, was named Duke (stadholder) by several provinces and was then made king. England and France sent soldiers to defend the new nation. In the end, the Catholic South became Belgium and the Protestant North became The Netherlands. The dukes of the House of Orange-Nassau became the royal family of The Netherlands.

The cities surrounding the Zuider Zee have the unusual aspect that they are largely invisible from the sea. The dikes are high enough so that houses and barns, which are mostly well below sea level, are rarely visible from the water. The homing beacon for the ships returning to the various ports became the steeple of the village or city church. Each city ended up having a church with a tall bell tower that was designed to be unique so as to identify the city to seamen on the water. The size of these large church towers was also meant to show the wealth of the city.

During the war against Spain cities fought each other bitterly. Cities aligned with Spain were Catholic and cities aligned with William of Orange were Calvinist Reformed, also known as Protestant. Atrocities took place on both sides. Catholic and Protestant refugees fled from city to city. Ships arriving from the sea urgently needed to know which side of the war controlled their destination. Many Protestant churches have a rooster on top of the steeple to this day to indicate "Calvinist" while Catholic churches have a cross. It was also customary to fly large flags from the steeples. Enkhuizen was not fought over and is still a city of Catholic, Lutheran and Reformed churches but other cities were fought over bitterly and became all Catholic or all Reformed.

"Near the harbor in Enkhuizen"
from a painting by Cornelis Springer

The Spanish left a great gift in West Friesland – the potato. The culture and consumption of potatoes changed life dramatically. Grain crops had been unreliable for centuries, producing years of good harvests and years of famine. When Spanish explorers brought back potatoes from South America, they were happily adopted by the Frisians. Potatoes grow well in Northern Europe and they became a staple food.

Imports from Asia and other far away lands came through the port of Antwerp until Spain conquered the city in 1585. The conquest gave the Portuguese and Spanish complete control of the trade in spices and other goods. Refugees from Antwerp brought knowledge and money to the cities of Holland and West Friesland producing a "gold rush" to outfit ships and take over the trades in silk, spices, cotton, silk and herbs. Ships were organized by entrepreneurs and manned by "companies". They were heavily armed for the task of taking over the foreign ports controlled by the Portuguese and Spanish. The ships were manned by rough men who fought among each other, attacked the overseas ports and competed fiercely for the trade. The Portuguese and Spanish ports on the Arabian Sea and the Indian Ocean were captured and held firmly in Dutch hands. The Spanish Armada was defeated by a Dutch and British fleet in 1588.

In 1602 the Parliament of the Seven Provinces intervened in the slaughter and forced the warring ship owners to join a centrally controlled group of independent local shipping companies called the Union of East India Companies. Each city organized a chamber of ship owners and sent representatives to the Union that became known as the Seventeen Lords. The cities whose "Lords" shared in control of the company were Amsterdam, Delft, Enkhuizen, Hoorn, Middelburg and Rotterdam. Enkhuizen had the largest number of shares.

The East India Companies were a huge success. Great riches were brought back to the port cities and a wonderful life resulted for all of the Netherlanders. This was the "Golden Age". Pepper was worth more than gold. Enkhuizen became very wealthy. Several city mints including one at Enkhuizen produced West Friesland daalder coinage for the use in Company controlled colonies. United States money is still called a "dollar". Ship construction became a major industry helped along by the invention in 1594 of a windmill powered sawmill that greatly improved shipbuilding efficiency. The shipbuilding ways located on the Wierdyk of Enkhuizen produced 108 large ships. Wood for the ships came from forests on the sand dunes and hills of Kennemerland along the English Channel. Alkmaar became a lumber city for the ship builders.

Ships departing for the high seas from Enkhuizen and other Zuider Zee ports left their port and went to anchorage near the island of Texel to await favorable winds. When the ships returned, they would go to another anchorage near the island of Wieringen. The heavily laden ships were too deep in the water to enter the shallow Zuider Zee and smaller ships would receive their cargo to bring it to port.

The anchorage at Wieringen served to isolate sailors on board the vessels returning from far away to make sure they did not bring diseases home with them. Doctors had no idea what caused most diseases but the concept of contagion was well understood. Sick sailors went to a hospital on the island and sometimes whole ships were kept at Wieringen for forty days to make sure that no sickness was brought home. The forty days of hospital or anchorage at Wieringen became known as the "quarantaine", which means forty days in French.

In 1607 Holland and West Friesland agreed to jointly fund draining one of the large lakes that was between them. The Beemster Lake was drained using 43 improved model windmill pumps to produce the first large polder in the North of Holland. The land averaged about twenty feet below sea level. By the year 1700, almost all the large lakes between Holland and West Friesland were drained and converted to farm land. Custom and language differences slowly faded and the ancient lands of Waterland, Kennemerland and West Friesland became North Holland while Holland became South Holland.

"Modern Enkhuizen, the Drommedaris in the foreground and the Zuider Kerk tower behind"

Enkhuizen started to decline about 1650. The fishery of the North Sea declined dramatically about 1625 and cod fishing failed completely from 1675 until 1704, apparently due to cooling of the sea. The city is not on a river that might keep a channel open to the sea. Large sand bars off the coast, named the "Enkhuizer Zand" started shifting so that even the smaller ships bringing riches from the anchorage at Wieringen had difficulty making the harbor. The cheese business declined with the loss of shipping. Other cities, Hoorn and notably Amsterdam received the riches instead. Wars at sea with Great Britain and Spain took their toll. The city had a population in 1630 of about 25,000 persons and was the third largest city after Haarlem and Amsterdam but a slow decline decreased this to about 5,000 in 1850. Fishing was still important but not enough to sustain the city. Many of the fabulous buildings including ship captains' houses on the Wierdyk and their warehouses for trade goods and pepper were dismantled and sold to merchants in Amsterdam. The large convent attached to the Zuider Kerk was also dismantled and sold. Between 1750 and 1850 about 1600 houses were torn down. The fleet diminished from about 400 ships to 10. The city walls and fortifications still stood while Enkhuizen became a poor fishing town that was isolated from the world and pretty well forgotten. Despite all the tearing down and poverty, the city still had much of its historic character and great civic pride in its history.

CHAPTER 2
WILLEM AND ANN

Willem

Near the city of Enkhuizen there are numerous little towns. The Enkhuizen harbor was constructed to be at sea level using surrounding dikes but the smaller towns had an opening in the dike with a lock to let the boats down into the local canals. The West Frisian word for a ship lock was sluys. In the twentieth century, most of the locks in the dikes were eliminated as the fisheries declined and the culture changed.

"Ysbrand Dirkszoon van ter Sluys" was born about 1750 in the very small town of Tersluys, located about one hour's walk South of Enkhuizen on the Westfriesian dike. In the West Frisian language his name was Ysbrand, the son of Dirk, from the Sluis. Surnames were not very common then and there was no regular custom for them. When the army of Napoleon took over West Friesland in 1806, all the farmers had to stand before a table of French soldiers and register for the census. Each man had to give a surname. Ysbrand picked the name Sluis and it was duly recorded. Some of the farmers thought it was all a joke and picked unmentionable words as their surname, expecting that the French would soon leave. The names recorded by the French Army are still the legal names of all their descendants even though the French left in 1815. Changing a family name under Dutch law is almost impossible.

The Sluis family ended up a few generations later in the town of Andyk, located about a two hour walk northwest of Enkhuizen. This town had land that was better drained and therefore more suitable for truck farming. The Sluis men were farmers who grew wheat, different kinds of cabbages and beans as well as caraway, mustard and anise seeds. The products were sold in nearby markets in Hoorn and Enkhuizen. Seed was saved from each year's crop for the following year. In time, some of the saved seed was sold to other farmers who had not saved their own. Several other families in Andyk were in the same business and competition sprang up to produce superior seed. The culture, breeding and development of vegetable seeds, and later flower seeds became an Andyk technology.

In the year 1867 two men, Nanne Sluis and Nanne Groot founded a seed company named "Sluis and Groot". The following year another company, "Sluis Brothers" was founded by Jacob and Pieter Sluis. The companies were located near each other just West of Enkhuizen. The Sluis and Groot families were in sometimes friendly competition and sometimes married each other. Growth of both companies was very good – so good that by 1910 all of the old remaining Enkhuizen warehouses of the East India Companies were filled with seed from "Sluis Brothers" and "Sluis and Groot". Export became important.

In 1883 the railroad came to Enkhuizen. The city had hoped for a financial renaissance but little happened. The city was at the end of the tracks that came from Amsterdam through Hoorn. A ferry ship connected the Enkhuizen rail head to a similar rail junction at Stavoren in Friesland across the Zuider Zee.

The Sluis family grew rapidly. The area near Enkhuizen was poor at the end of the nineteenth century with bad prospects for the farmers. Many Andyk men and women decided to go to America for better opportunities, they took their seed skills with them. Thousands of West Frieslanders emigrated to the United States. Orange City, Iowa and Chicago, Illinois were often their destinations.

In 1908 Joost Sluis, son of Pieter Sluis was the Director of the Sluis Brothers seed company in Enkhuizen. He sent his oldest son Jacob to Chicago to work at a branch of the Enkhuizen Company that was started to get better access to the American market. Joost's brother Nanne was running the store in Chicago at 544 West 63rd Street on the very edge of the city with Joost's son Siebe working in the store. Siebe's 20 year old brother Jacob soon began traveling as a salesman to sell Enkhuizen seed in the U.S. The "Sluis Seed Store" did business with seed companies established by men from Andyk in Iowa, Wisconsin, North Dakota, Washington and California. Jacob's uncle Nanne sold seed to local gardeners in the Chicago area. In 1912, Nanne left to start his own seed business, "N. Sluis and Son"

Jacob married a first cousin, Nanne's daughter Maritje Sluis on May 11, 1910 in Racine, Wisconsin. Maritje and Jacob had four children, Joost in 1910, Mary in 1913, Willem on January 19, 1915 and a second child named Joost in 1917. The first child named Joost died at the age of six, just before the last of the four children was born so the new baby received the same name. Jacob's father Joost suddenly died in March, 1917. Maritje, Jacob's wife, died in Chicago from the Spanish Influenza in 1918 as a victim of the great world wide epidemic that killed millions.

On December 19, 1918, Jacob's brother Bram wrote that Jacob should return home in order to help run the family business. Jacob had more experience than his younger brothers and he returned to Enkhuizen in the spring of 1919 as a 30 year old widower with his three surviving children. At first he lived in the house his father had lived in. Jacob remarried in September, 1919 with Aafje Groot. Jacob and Aafje would have six more children: Simon, Alida, Jan, Jacob, Klaas and Margaret.

"The Enkhuizen house Jacob Sluis returned to from Chicago in 1919"

The Sluis Seed Store in Chicago became obsolete when Jacob continued to export seed from the company in Holland and found that the trade could be managed without having a base in the United States. Sales visits to American buyers were made directly from Holland. The store was closed when the manager left in 1923. Jacob's brother Siebe started another independent seed store in Chicago, "Sluis Seed" at 7219 South Halsted Street.

The Sluis Brothers seed company in North Holland became very successful. Together with other seed companies, the business greatly improved the economy of Enkhuizen. Jacob became the single head of the business and groomed his oldest son Willem to take over when the time came. The Jacob Sluis family lived in the middle of Enkhuizen in a large house on the main street, called the West Street or "Westerstraat". The Westerstraat had originally connected the two towns of Enchusae and Gommerskerspel. The street led from near the "South Church" to the "West Church" of the city, and then went West to the "Cow Gate" and out of town to the seed farms.

Willem was a sensitive young man with artistic temperament. At his father's direction, Willem observed the seed trial fields near company headquarters to learn about the business while in school. When he completed college, he was sent to England for a half year to work in greenhouses that were experimenting with radiation induced mutation to try for better seed varieties. His English improved during his stay in England but he was never convinced that the radiation method of altering genetics had much value.

After England, Willem was sent to a seed growing division of the Sluis Brothers Company at Saint Remy-De-Provence in France for a year. His French improved there, he learned a lot about the business and he made several lifelong friends. Willem was joined there for a time by his brother Joost, the two shared friendships and experiences.

Starting in the mid 1930's, Willem traveled throughout Europe and in America as a salesman for the family business as his father had done. As an American citizen born in Chicago, he was well received in the United States.

Ann

Bernard Kuiper married his much younger wife Lena Buis in 1911. The couple lived in a small rented row house at Paulus Potter Street 15 in Enkhuizen. The couple had a son, Cornelis, in 1913 and then a daughter, Ann, on February 21, 1915. Sister Mary was born in 1918.

Ann was a very weak baby, so much so that when grandfather Buis held her he stated "That one won't last".

Bernard was in the coal business with his father and a very

hard worker. His business consisted largely of selling anthracite coal by the bag to the citizens of Enkhuizen. The very poor could not afford the imported German hard coal, so he also sold wood and blocks of peat cut from the swamps that served as a poor substitute. His coal wagon made regular rounds through the city delivering coal and peat. He was generous with credit and charity to the poor and was a respected business man.

In 1918, Bernard moved into his father's house that stood on the dike of the original inner harbor of Enkhuizen. The house stood at the end of the long, narrow old harbor, overlooking it and facing directly East so as to have a clear view of the "Drommedaris" and the bend in the harbor entrance at the other end. Three old gabled warehouses remaining from the East India Companies stood on the South side of the harbor near the Kuiper house. The house still had bedsteads in the attic with their straw insulation and doors that could be closed at night to keep in the heat of those asleep in the bed. The front of the house stood on the inner harbor dike while the back of the house was lower on the back of the dike. It was a house with a "walk out basement". The back yard sloped downward to a small canal whose water was about fifteen feet lower than the water in the harbor in front of the house. Bernard's business had old coal and peat warehouses next to the house on the dike and a horse barn a short distance away for draft horses. Boats laden with bricks of peat cut from the bogs unloaded in the harbor across the street from the house and sheds. The street next to the house steeply sloped downward from the dike into the city. The dike was called the "Kuiper's Dike".

Bernard was a forward looking man. His house on the Kuiper's Dike was the first house in Enkhuizen with electric light and Lena Kuiper was the first woman in West Friesland to acquire an electric washing machine. The townspeople all had to come and look at the newest technological wonders.

Contrary to grandpa Buis' expectations, Ann grew up to be a strong and feisty daughter. Ann was outgoing while her sister Mary was happier at home. Mary was more like mother Lena so that Ann became allied with father while Mary was mom's girl. Ann was athletic and ambitious, played the piano and the violin, went on bike trips with her girlfriends, and had a lot of friends all over the city, then of about 10,000 people. Father Bernard doted on her and she could manipulate him well. The family thrived.

Ann was adventurous and would often sneak away from home to be seen swimming at the harbor entrance of the town with the boys in the dangerous chop of the North Sea. In 1927 the Zuider Zee froze hard. Twelve year old Ann scared all of her relatives by riding her bicycle over the sea ice to the island of Urk.

Ann was an avid reader who dreamed of traveling the world someday and she did not like house work. In 1928 she decided that she needed to become a businesswoman. Mother Lena was of the old fashioned opinion that women did not need school and would not give permission. Ann went to father Bernard, who overruled his wife and permitted Ann to attend night school in business. She graduated in 1931 with a diploma in business that included certification in French, English and German business correspondence

"Ann's business school diploma"

"Ann as a young woman"

At about this time, the City of Enkhuizen renamed the portion of the dike street on which the Kuiper house stood from "Kuiper's Dyk" to "Waaigat", which means "windy place". Bernard Kuiper was not pleased with the new address: Waaigat 2.

Ann's violin lessons were from the same teacher who taught Willem Sluis. They became acquainted. Willem was a star student while Ann did well.

Willem and Ann

North Holland had suffered another of its terrible floods on January 14, 1916. Enkhuizen was not affected directly but much of the land of West Friesland and other parts of Netherlands were flooded when the dikes were breached by storm waters and high winds. The disaster caused serious consideration of a dam that would once and for all protect the North of the Netherlands from flooding by the North Sea. World War I put the project on hold but the Parliament and Queen Wilhelmina authorized the project. Construction took place in the 1920's and was completed in 1932. Queen Wilhelmina visited Enkhuizen in 1930!

The great Closure Dike started in the west at the shallow water where the island of Wieringen had once been and ended in Friesland on the eastern side of the Zuider Zee. Known as the "Afsluitdyk", the great dike made Holland safer. A great celebration in the cities on the Zuider Zee was held at the official opening in September, 1933. Eighteen year olds Ann and Willem took part in the fun and the great excursion to see the newest wonder.

The Closure Dike made Enkhuizen an inland city. The fishery started to decline and change although it was possible to go to the North Sea through locks in the great dike. The Zuider Zee no longer received salt water from the Atlantic and slowly turned into a fresh water lake with the Ysel River as its main water source. The Zuider Zee was renamed the Ysel Lake. The river "Y" had earlier been turned into a canal.

In 1937, Willem Sluis won an annual violin competition that had as its prize the honor of playing First Violin with the Concertgebouw Orchestra in Amsterdam. Jacob was very proud of his son and bought him a concert violin for the event. The violin was carefully kept in its case throughout his life.

Ann had various boyfriends. She once confided that when a boy and girl went on the seaward side of a dike they had wonderful privacy. The dikes normally had long grass growing on them and cows grazing. Other suitors were rejected, though, because Ann had her heart set on the glamorous world traveler from the richest family in the city.

22 • COMING TO MOKENA

"Willem Sluis, official Sluis Brothers photo, 1937"

Ann and Willem became engaged to be married in April, 1938. Formal announcements were published by the church and by all the newspapers. The families formally met, had portraits made, and became acquainted. The couple had a few months together and then father Jacob Sluis sent Willem to the United States to sell seed. Willem was familiar with American seed customers such as Burpee, Ball and others and had a very successful sales trip. When planning his return, he bought a 1938 Chevrolet Coupe and had it shipped to The Netherlands on the ship that brought him back home. The car was very modern looking, one of the first cars made with am aerodynamic shape. On arrival in Rotterdam, he took the car to Enkhuizen and caused a sensation. No one had ever seen such a car!

The wedding took place on May 19, 1939. Black automobiles were brought in from several towns and companies to serve as limousines. Automobiles were a very rare luxury. Enkhuizen was physically small inside its ancient walls so that walking was the normal way to get around. Few people owned automobiles. Truck drivers from the Sluis Brothers and other seed companies drove the cars.

The wedding was a huge society event. The limousines first picked up the bride, her bridesmaids and family at the Kuiper house, where scores of townspeople came to watch, and then went to the sixteenth century city hall for the formal civil marriage. The groom's family came with more limousines from the Sluis home on the Westerstraat. The Mayor of Enkhuizen officiated.

"Willem and Ann marry"

After the civil wedding, the entire entourage went by limousine to the Christian Reformed Church on the Klopper Street for the church wedding. The church was packed with people and hundreds waited outside. The formal church wedding was then followed by another limousine ride to the wedding reception.

Traveling salesmen have had a bad name for centuries. In the sixteenth century, the city of Cleve in Western Germany sent salesmen all over Europe. They were not trusted and often had a difficult time finding a place to stay, which caused many cities to have a hotel or guest house with the name Cleve in it to let the salesmen know they were welcome. "Die Port Van Cleve" was the only hotel in Enkhuizen in 1939. The hotel was so old that it had been built by shipwrights and had large timbers visible in all the rooms. In 1939 the main customers were visitors to the seed companies west of the city. The Sluis wedding reception was held in the hotel ballroom.

"Hotel Die Port Van Cleve"

Willem and Ann had a fabulous honeymoon. The couple drove to Paris with the Chevrolet coupe and spent several days there being feted by managers of Sluis Brothers affiliates, then to Saint

Remy-De-Provence where Willem showed off his new bride. While at Saint Remy, the pair was given a set of two 70MM artillery shells that had been converted into vases by artists in the trenches of World War I. The vases were made by hammering the powder cases from the inside to raise the images of roses and leaves. They became family treasures that stayed with Ann throughout her life and always occupied a place of honor in her home. A week on the Riviera in luxury hotels and spas, a stop in Monte Carlo and then a trip through Northern Italy and the Alps returned them home. The marriage was off to a wonderful start.

"The Riviera"

Willem had bought a modern house in the city and had it remodeled. The house was on a street still named "Spanish Army" after the Spanish garrison that had been located there centuries before. The house had a large back yard and was named "Ons Genoegen", which means Our Satisfaction or Pleasure. The name of the house was in a large stone above the door. A canal ran along the brick street in front of the house.

The house was filled with the latest furnishings from Germany's designers. The living room and bedroom furniture had built in indirect lighting which was wonderfully modern at the time. The bedroom set was veneered in birch burl with a blonde finish. A buffet cabinet in the living room had a built in lighted bar. The concept of a "coffee table" in the living room was brand new at that time – the coffee table also had indirect lighting. With the best china service, sterling silver flatware, wonderful linens, and beautiful decorations all was modern and luxurious. A new piano was installed. When the couple moved in, the house became a fun gathering place for the family with Willem and Ann playing violin together and Ann playing the piano for all.

At the time of the wedding, father Jacob had appointed Willem to be Assistant Director of the Sluis Brothers seed company. After the honeymoon, Willem went to work with his father. The two did not get along well. Willem accused his father of excessively sharp business dealings with seed farmers and other misdeeds that caused the two to split. In early 1940, Willem and his father finally separated from each other. Willem demanded that he be given his share of Sluis Brothers so that he could start up a seed company of his own. An agreement was made with both Willem and his brother Joost. The two brothers bought a seed company in the city of Delft named Zwaan and Co. which they would run as partners. Willem also bought a house in Delft and put his Enkhuizen house up for sale. Willem's half brother Simon took Willem's place at Sluis Brothers. Simon would become the Director in 1951 when Jacob retired. Under Simon's leadership the Sluis Brothers seed company would become world famous.

Ann, in the meantime, had become pregnant with her first child. She had a wonderful life at Ons Genoegen but found to her dismay that some of her many girl friends would not talk to her any more. Holland still had strong class distinctions at that time and Ann had moved to the upper class. Men of the lower class still tipped their caps when their "seniors" passed. Clothing for wear in public was distinctive by class and the upper classes were expected to dress formally. Class distinctions did not exist among single girls but married women were addressed in accordance with their rank in society. Some of the girls who had married ordinary men no longer felt comfortable with Ann and became unavailable to her.

In the spring of 1940, Willem was traveling back and forth between Enkhuizen and Delft, arranging for the move, planning his new company and awaiting the birth of his firstborn.

CHAPTER 3
WAR

On May 10, 1940, disaster struck in the form of the German Army. The Netherlands military had mobilized its reserves in the fall of 1939, expecting war. They were poorly equipped for the German "Blitzkrieg" with fast tank forces and air assaults. The defense plan of The Netherlands depended on flooding land along the Rhine and Ysel rivers but the attack was so rapid that it could not be implemented. German armor rapidly captured the eastern areas of the country but then slowed due to blown bridges and flooded areas. Paratroopers landed in various places, capturing bridges and strong points.

The Dutch had learned from the German assault on Norway earlier that year. In Norway, troop transport planes had simply landed unannounced on various airfields to deliver soldiers. Netherlands forces rapidly placed obstacles on airfield runways with the result that many German troop transport planes crashed on landing. Half of the "Junkers" tri-motor troop transport planes of the German air force were destroyed on the ground or shot down. In Rotterdam, at The Hague and elsewhere, the Netherlands Army put up a strong defense that stopped the assault. German troop losses were heavy. Rotterdam was defended and held by a badly equipped but capably led force. German paratroops captured the Rhine river bridges at the city of Moerdyk south of Rotterdam and were able to stop a gallant French division that had raced northward to defend the city.

The strong defense of the Netherlands shocked and infuriated the German High Command. An ultimatum was given to surrender or face bombing of the cities. Queen Wilhelmina fled to England

and ordered the army holding Rotterdam to surrender. The surrender was arranged and signed on May 14, 1940 but the German Luftwaffe was already in the air during the signing and was not called back. Hundreds of German planes then bombed the center of Rotterdam in a treacherous aerial attack that outraged the world. The ancient city with its magnificent sixteenth and seventeenth century buildings was burned to the ground. After threats to bomb other cities were made, The Netherlands formally surrendered on May 15. A battalion of brave soldiers defending the heavily fortified Closure Dike and another group holding The Hague had to give up. Small groups fought the Germans for almost a month more. The Netherlands became an occupied vassal state.

Willem was in Delft but rushed home to Enkhuizen, driving on country roads to avoid the shooting. A telephone call from the American Embassy advised him to leave The Netherlands at once with Americans that were being evacuated. The Americans said that only he could go – his wife was not an American. Willem stayed with his wife.

On June 6, 1940 Ann went into labor. Willem had made some arrangements for Ann to deliver her child at home. The hospitals were filled with German wounded and were reserved for the military. Willem took the dining room table and placed it in the center of the first floor, away from the windows, because there was still fear of bombing near Enkhuizen. A mattress was placed on the table to make a bed. The second floor was thought to be too dangerous.

Ann was in labor for three days. There was no doctor available since the German Army had requisitioned them all. On the evening of June 9, Doctor Keyer, the family physician, was given leave from the hospital for a night's sleep at home. He heard of Ann's plight and came to Ons Genoegen where he delivered Joost with forceps and the little he had in his bag at 1 AM. It was a breech birth that had caused the lengthy labor. Joost and Ann barely survived. Joost had major scars on his head from being turned with forceps. The scars were later repaired by drawing the skin of his head together, leaving a single spot.

In October, 1940, Willem and Ann with their four month old boy moved to Delft. Willem had been able to purchase a modern row house that had been built in the 1930's just outside the old city walls. The house was thoroughly up to date for the time. The furniture was brought from Enkhuizen and set up. The address was "Fransen Van de Putten Straat 22". Ann busied herself with her baby and Willem was hard at work with the new business.

"The Sluis house in Delft"

Ann's new house was nicely located a short walk from the center of the city. It was a twenty minute walk to the central square with its "new" church where William of Orange and the royal family are buried. The central square was home to the weekly market with hundreds of stalls selling produce and other items. The more sophisticated shopping stores of the city were also close. The family attended church in the "old" church, completed in 1350, ten minutes walk from home.

The house in Delft, like the house in Enkhuizen, was a happy house that was popular with Willem's brothers. Willem's younger brother Joost was his business partner and lived with the family. Brother Jan frequently came to visit. Ann played the piano well and all would sing and enjoy life together. Joost was serious minded while Willem had a wry humor. Jan was a story teller and fun to be around.

"In the new house"

Joost

Willem's brother Joost was a cadet in the Netherlands Military. When the German occupation was fully established, he determined that he should flee Holland to fight for the liberation of the Fatherland. He led the seed company with Willem until July, 1941 when he left Delft. The business was not going well because of the war. Willem stayed with his family and with the business.

Joost, together with a friend named Rian Collee and two other men decided to escape Netherlands and go to England. The first attempt was a trip to Hoek Van Holland which is West of Rotterdam at the mouth of the Rhine River. There security was too tight and they abandoned the attempt. Another attempt was made, this time to reach the border of Spain with France. The four men reached Perpignan near the French border and started to look for a guide to lead them to Spain. The men determined that the Netherlands consul in the area was probably a German sympathizer and abandoned this attempt as too dangerous.

After the failed attempt to cross into Spain, Joost and the other men spent a few months at the Sluis Brothers farm in Saint Remy-De-Provence. While there they decided to make another attempt by crossing into Switzerland near Annemasse. Joost and Rian Collee made it to Geneva but two men who tried to cross with them were arrested at the border by the Germans and sent to a concentration camp where one of them eventually died.

In Geneva Joost and Rian met Guup Krayenhoff who was a student there. Guup did not want to go back to The Netherlands and the three of them got along well. The three men decided to try to reach England together.

Joost had a serious demeanor and could pass for a much older man than his 24 years. The group was able to obtain false passports and Joost's said he was 50 years old. Guup was actually 19 but his new passport showed him as 16. The Netherlands military attaché in Bern helped with the project. The three made it by train to Portugal and then found a ship that took them to England with some Belgians and other Netherlanders.

The English screened all the arrivals. Some of them ended up in the secret service and were later dropped by parachute into Holland where many of them were betrayed to the Germans. They became victims of the famous "Englandspiel" of the German Secret Service. Two men in the group were determined to be German spies – they were hanged in the Tower of London.

Joost, Rian and Guup wanted action and reported for training as fighter pilots. Joost and Rian were already reserve officers in the Netherlands Royal Army and were officially on active duty since the German invasion of The Netherlands in May, 1940. They were attached to a Netherlands Detachment in London on January 4, 1942.

"Joost with his bombardier wings"

Joost had studied economics and was assigned to a desk job in that field. He refused the job because he wanted active service. Guup Krayenhoff, who was new to the military, was sent to Wolverhampton for basic training.

On May 11, 1942 Joost was commissioned as a Reserve First Lieutenant in the Royal Air Force Volunteer Reserve. He was sent to Canada for pilot training with Guup. Joost ended up being rejected for pilot training and was then sent to Jackson, Mississippi for training as bombardier. He graduated on August 6, 1943 and received his bombardier wings.

Joost and Rian were assigned to the 320th Squadron of the Royal Air Force. The 320th was the Netherlands Squadron of bombers, under Netherlands Command. The squadron planes were marked with an orange triangle for the House of Orange-Nassau. Rian was a pilot and Joost ultimately became the wing bombardier of the squadron. The squadron originally flew "Hudson" bombers but was provided with B-25 "Mitchell" bombers in early 1944.

Joost flew 38 missions with the squadron from the RAF field at Dunsfold, England. On February 24, 1944, while bombing a command post for V-1 Flying Bombs at Chateau D'Ansenne in France, Joost's plane was struck in an engine and fell to earth. The entire crew perished and all were buried in the church cemetery of Saint Remy-De-Boscrocourt.

Jan

Willem's half brother Jan was born in Enkhuizen in 1924. At the start of the war he was just sixteen years old. He liked to visit and stay at the Sluis house in Delft and met a girl friend there in the form of Ann's maid, Molly Pieterse. Jan and Molly hit it off very well to the extent that Willem and Ann let Molly go after a time because they were concerned that the romance might go out of control. Jan then started to visit the Pieterse house near Rotterdam where he met his eventual wife, Molly's sister Cornelia.

The underground movement against the Germans was especially active in Rotterdam and nearby Delft because of the bombing of May, 1940. Jan was active in the underground movement and was hidden at the Sluis home in Delft on several occasions. Willem and Ann quietly supported the resistance. He was eventually arrested by the Germans and sent to the concentration camp at

Amersfoort from spring, 1943 until spring, 1944. The details of his release from the camp are not clear. One story is that Father Jacob in Enkhuizen was able to bribe the guards to let him go. The story told by Willem later was that Jan said that he had become very sick in the camp, was thrown out in a field as dying and was then nursed back to health by a friendly farmer. In any case, he survived the camp and was able to hide until the liberation of Southern Netherlands in the summer of 1944. His health remained precarious for the rest of his life. After the war, Jan made six or seven visits to the Sluis house in Delft where his story telling endeared him to the children.

"Jan"

Jan later emigrated to the United States. He homesteaded in Alaska and stayed there for three years but found that the weather was too hard for him. He then moved to Seattle for a time. Jan traveled to The Netherlands to marry his Cornelia before settling in California where he was the manager of a grocery store. Jan died in 1990.

The War Bites In

When Joost left The Netherlands to try for England, he was registered with the police as a resident of the Sluis home in Delft. The Germans were very thorough in their record keeping and noticed after a short while that he had not appeared to get a new food ration card. Ann was called to the police station to explain. She later explained that if she had not been strong enough to stick to her story, she would have been gone. She would not explain what the story was but she was held for two days.

Food rationing started in 1941. At first it was fairly benign, controlling the amount of butter, sugar and meat that could be purchased per person. As the needs of the German Wehrmacht increased, the food available to the civilian populations decreased, especially in the occupied states. Everyone had been issued a ration card and an official identification card. Both cards were essential since without them no food could be purchased and arrest was automatic if no identification card was presented when demanded by police or military personnel.

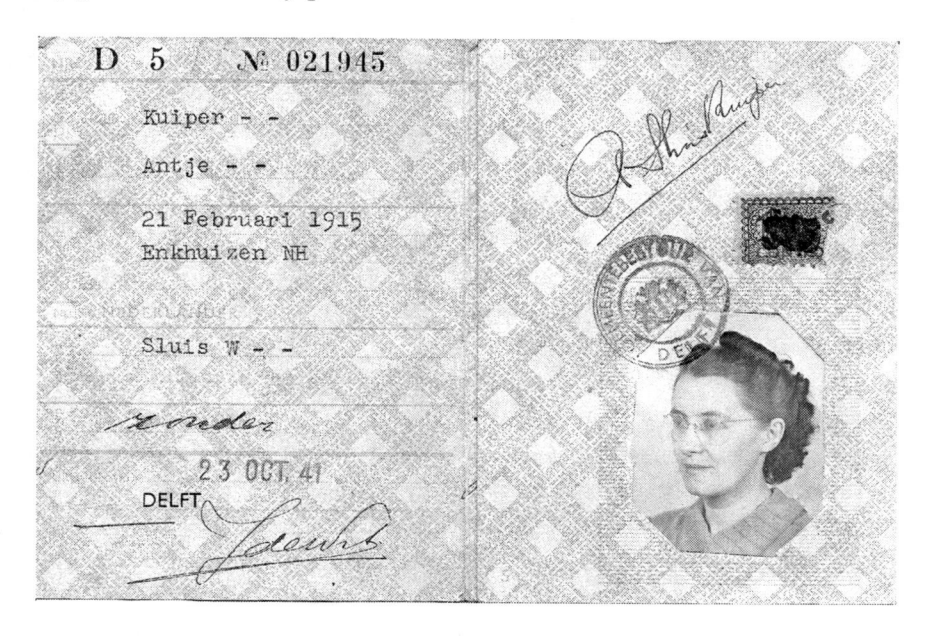

"Ann's identification card"

The German Occupation Army went to great lengths to try to convince the Dutch of their good fortune in being part of the Third Reich. Military bands played lovely concerts. Germany installed a copy of its ruling N.D.S.A.P. National German Socialist Workers Party in The Netherlands. The Socialist Workers Party promised utopia with free medical care for all, free education, strict government control of business and trade, wonderful youth programs, humane euthanasia and abortion for the incurable or unwanted, control of the purity of the race through eugenics, and a lot of other scientific benefits. Voluntary community service was encouraged. Religion was officially protected but was banished from the public realm as not compatible with the Darwinist atheism of the ruling elites. About twenty thousand Netherlanders were convinced enough to join the German Army. There were many who had secretly supported the German cause. The majority, however, considered the Germans, as always, as the uncivilized savages from the east who could not be trusted. The well educated Dutch had been watching Germany for many years and wanted no part of the "new order". Posters and placards advertising the glories of the new order were everywhere to be seen but had little effect.

The Germans confiscated most of the automobiles but there was almost no gasoline ration anymore anyway. Businesses that had to deliver goods could still operate in a restricted way. Willem still had an automobile and a gasoline ration since he claimed to need it for business.

Aluminum cookware had become available as a new luxury in the late 1930's and was treasured by many cooks. All aluminum articles were confiscated during the summer of 1941 for use in aircraft production.

Another order required that all prewar radios had to be turned in to the authorities. The Netherlands had a "radio tax" that had to be paid for every radio. The radios were therefore licensed which made it easy for the Germans to identify almost all the radios in the country. The only radios left after a short collection period were those that had not been legally licensed before the war. New radios could be purchased that only received government stations.

Possession of any type of weapon was illegal. Guns were rare in prewar Holland and had also been licensed which made them easy to gather up. Members of the resistance had been able to hide some military weapons. Possession of weapons was made a capital crime.

Helen was born on February 9, 1942. The family was happy and able to celebrate the birth of a daughter. A proud trip was made to Enkhuizen to show off the baby.

The cities were under martial law. Persons convicted of crimes were routinely sentenced to a new form of rehabilitation called "national service" and sent to work camps. Democratic processes were routinely overruled by politicized courts. Socialist Worker Party judges now ruled and made new laws making ordinary activities such as criticism of the government a crime. Some persons were sent to the camps simply because of their ancestry. Vagrancy was a work camp crime and persons who were unshaven or were badly dressed were routinely arrested. Telephone calls were monitored. Spies were known to attend churches to report opposition to the government. Neighbors spied on each other. People disappeared. The piano and violins were heard less often.

The town homes on the Fransen van de Putten Straat had back yards that were surrounded by a six foot wooden fence. Along the back of all the yards a narrow alley ran parallel to the street, separating the yards of one street from those of another. A small gate from each back yard gave access to the alley. German patrols were aware of these and would send a soldier to look into the alley while patrolling the street. Willem made a secret door between his yard and the neighbors to permit escape if needed.

Willem faithfully paid his employees until the fall of 1942 when a German army truck pulled up to the Sluis Seed Company in Delft, took most of the seed and supplies and confiscated all assets of the company without giving a receipt. The Sluis automobile and all bank accounts were taken. The Willem and Joost Sluis fortune was now destroyed. Willem still had the building and some sacks of seed that had been left behind.

BEVEL.

Op bevel der Duitsche Weermacht moeten alle mannen in den leeftijd van 17 t/m 40 jaar zich voor den arbeidsinzet aanmelden.

Hiervoor moeten ALLE mannen van dezen leeftijd onmiddellijk na ontvangst van dit bevel met de voorgeschreven uitrusting op straat gaan staan.

Alle andere bewoners, ook vrouwen en kinderen, moeten in de huizen blijven totdat de actie ten einde is. De mannen van de genoemde jaargangen, die bij een huiszoeking nog in huis worden aangetroffen, worden gestraft, waarbij hun particulier eigendom zal worden aangesproken.

Bewijzen van vrijstelling van burgerlijke of militaire instanties moeten ter contrôle worden meegebracht. Ook zij, die in het bezit zijn van zulke bewijzen, zijn verplicht zich op straat te begeven.

Er moeten worden medegebracht: warme kleeding, stevige schoenen, dekens, bescherming tegen regen, eetgerei, mes, vork, lepe, drinkbeker en boterhammen voor één dag.

De dagelijksche vergoeding bestaat uit goeden kost, rookartikelen en loon volgens het geldende tarief.

Voor de achterblijvende familieleden zal worden gezorgd.

Het is aan alle bewoners der gemeente verboden hun woonplaats te verlaten.

Op hen, die pogen te ontvluchten of weerstand te bieden, zal worden geschoten.

(Translation)

COMMAND.

BY COMMAND of the **GERMAN ARMY** all men of the ages 17 to 40 years inclusive must report themselves for special labor service.

ALL men of these ages must immediately on receipt of this command go to the street and wait for orders with the specified equipment.

All other citizens, also women and children, must stay in their houses until this action is ended. Men of the specified ages who are found in the houses when they are searched will be punished and their personal property will be confiscated.

PERMITS OF EXEMPTION from civilian or military sources must be brought along. Men who are in possession of such permits must also stand on the street.

EQUIPMENT THAT MUST BE BROUGHT: Warm clothing, strong shoes, blankets, rain gear, eating utensils, a knife, fork and spoon, a drinking cup and sandwiches for one day.

DAILY COMPENSATION WILL CONSIST OF GOOD FOOD, SMOKING ARTICLES, AND PAY IN ACCORDANCE WITH THE APPLICABLE TARRIF
THE FAMILIES LEFT BEHIND WILL BE CARED FOR.

ALL MEMBERS OF THE COMMUNITY ARE FORBIDDEN TO LEAVE THEIR RESIDENCES

THOSE WHO TRY TO FLEE OR RESIST WILL BE SHOT

(Distributed in Delft, The Netherlands during May, 1943)

CHAPTER 4
AGONY

In the spring of 1943 German soldiers came door to door with a command from the occupation army that all men aged 16 through 40 had to report for labor duty at once. Families left behind would be well cared for. Those who resisted would be shot.

Not one person believed the promises that were made in the order. The men did not want to leave their wives and children to the tender care of the German Army and did not expect to return home if they went. National service was understood to be nothing but slave labor.

Willem and Ann had developed a plan. The town house in Delft had a dry crawl space under the first floor that had a concrete floor and a ceiling height of about two and a half feet. Word had spread from Amsterdam that the order was coming. The crawl space was already equipped with mattresses. It had an electric light. A prewar radio had been in the crawl space since 1941. When the Germans came to take the men, five men were rapidly hidden under the house. They would stay there on and off for eighteen months. They could not stand or sit upright. Signals were devised that consisted of pounding on the floor to warn of danger.

Ann was brave. The men hidden under the house were a constant source of worry. Whenever it was judged to be safe, Ann would move the heavy furniture that stood on the rug that covered the hatch to the crawl space. She would open up the hatch. The men would come out or food would be passed down. Ann was careful not to let her children see the access. It was always carefully put back exactly as before.

The men did not officially exist and had no food ration because of it. Trusted neighbors helped smuggle food to the Sluis house for the men, gleaned from their meager rations. Two of the men were Protestant, one was Jewish and two were Roman Catholic. The Parish Priest was aware of the situation and helped with the food operation. Men could no longer attend church.

The German occupation forces were very thorough. Birth records were collected from all cities and carefully searched for Jewish and other officially defective citizens. Undesirable citizens were then arrested for "relocation" or "national service". The Jewish man under the house was neighbor Toon (Tony) Brokx. Tony was a teacher who read German periodicals and realized before the war that the Germans might come after him. He successfully had his records changed in the Delft city hall and the school where he taught so that he remained undetected during the war. Had he gone to a work camp, things might have been different.

In late summer of 1943, Ann underwent another round of interrogation by the police. She survived again.

In the fall of 1943, a German patrol searched door to door looking for escaped workers. Ann knew they were coming and quickly placed a galvanized wash tub in the kitchen and filled it with water. She then scared son Joost by telling him that the German soldiers were coming to get him. Joost believed that his father had been taken away and was very afraid. When the Germans arrived, they found Ann bathing her little baby daughter Helen in the kitchen and a little three year old boy crying in the little half bath under the stairs. Stories circulated that the Germans would shoot through the floor if they suspected something amiss. The soldiers were charmed by the scene and distracted by the little boy crying in the bathroom. The five men under the floor were spared.

AGONY · 43

"Little Helen in her tub"

During the winter of 1943-1944 electricity became a rarity. The city used gas made from coal, which also stopped. The kitchen stove of the Sluis house was made for gas but a worker from Willem's company was able to make it work with wood or coal. The windows of the houses were covered with black paper to make sure that no light could escape to the outside from the candles sometimes used for light. Neighbors helped each other by looking for light leaks. No one was allowed outside at night. German patrols would shoot at light that was escaping from a house or arrest the occupants. Delft was cold, dark and hungry. The regular newspapers were controlled by the government and could not be trusted. Illegal underground newspapers printed on small pieces of paper were slipped to trusted friends. The very brave engaged in the dangerous practice of listening to the unlawful prewar radios for the "BBC" when there was electricity. Ann and Willem supported each other through it all. Willem knew just how to cheer Ann up with his humor when she needed it and Ann knew how to give Willem more courage. They were strong together.

Willem Jr. was born on February 13, 1944.

Willem sneaked out of the crawl space often enough to help keep the family going. The Germans had missed taking some bean seed at his seed business but it was not edible because it had been treated with a fungicide. Willem found that soaking the beans in water and rubbing them dry would remove visible traces of the fungicide. The beans were eaten. Sugar beets turned out to be barely edible. Willem had made lamps out of some small pieces of cork, some wire and candle wicks. A "y" of wire was suspended by three pieces of cork to hold a wick located at the junction. Oil that Willem pressed from seed was burned to provide dim lighting at night after the candles were gone.

In those days, men shaved with double edge razor blades but they were no longer obtainable. It turned out to be possible to sharpen the blades by rubbing them against the inside of a water glass. A few enterprising men made charcoal burners that would produce a poor coal gas fuel that could power the few cars and trucks that were left. A few very smelly coal gas fueled cars were seen. Life slowed to a crawl. Old cigarette butts became a valuable trade commodity. A small scrap of soap was a treasured gift.

In August, 1944, the local Parish Priest was arrested and sent to a German camp. A spy reported him for speaking against the government. The underground newspapers had reported that priests and ministers that would not conform were sent to Bavaria to a place called Dachau. Ann was not Catholic, but the Priest wanted to honor her as a courageous Christian woman. He thanked her by giving his rosary to a woman of the Parish with instructions to deliver it to Ann. He joined the thousands of priests and ministers who did not return. The rosary is a family treasure.

On the Western side of Delft, near The Hague, there was an air base called Ypenburg. This base was used by the Netherlands Royal Air Force for aircraft before the war, but now was used by the Germans as a launching base for V-1 "Buzz Bombs" to bomb Great Britain and for fighters. Willem's brother Joost was killed bombing just such a place in France. The V-1 was a crude jet engine that made a loud whirring noise with a winged bomb hung underneath. They did not always work as designed. Late in 1944 one of these devices went wrong over the City of Delft and crashed into the Sluis Seed Company, badly damaging the building. Willem's Delft dream was now impossible.

The citizens of Delft were subject to frequent air raid sirens. The old city of Delft was not heavily bombed but no one could know where the bombs would land next. Bombs were frequently heard as factories, railroads and the air base at Ypenburg nearby were bombed with regularity. The port of Rotterdam, fifteen miles to the south, was also bombed often. Fighter planes screamed into the sky constantly. In the daytime, large formations of planes could sometimes be seen heading east toward Germany. Antiaircraft guns near Delft were active day and night. Spent shells from the guns fell on the city. When people were hit by falling debris there was no longer formal medical care for them.

In September, 1944, British and American forces tried to gain control of the Rhine River bridges in The Netherlands. Paratroopers landed near each of the main bridges and fought valiantly to capture them but the attempt at Arnhem failed. The Dutch underground supported the attack by stopping all rail traffic into and out of the battle zone. The Germans were wild with rage. In retaliation, all rail traffic into and out of Western Netherlands was stopped and remained stopped for the rest of the war. The trains disappeared into Germany.

The people of Delft knew about the attempt to capture the Rhine River bridges and were filled with hope. The liberation of Antwerp in Belgium was common knowledge. Enough news filtered to the people through illegal radios and underground newspapers so that liberation seemed near. The failure at Arnhem and the resulting cutoff of supplies was terrifying.

Delft now starved, along with all of the western part of The Netherlands. No more food. No more fuel. The city was cold and dark that winter. All the trees along the streets were cut down. Parks kept their trees because of police patrols. The pets all disappeared into cooking pots along with all the rats. Going out in public was extremely dangerous. Those forced to use public transportation came home infested with lice and fleas. People were dying in the streets. The German army was rarely seen and it became safer for the crawl space men to move about. The Sluis children saw their father again. People were scavenging for coal that had fallen from steam locomotives by walking along the railroad tracks. Those who were caught were shot as saboteurs even though there were no more trains..

One day all those living near the railroad were ordered out of their houses to watch the execution of four men who had been arrested. Between the Sluis home and Delft there was a canal that had been the moat of the city. The railroad ran along the moat. A railroad crossing and bridge were the normal route into the city for shopping. All the women and children were forced to watch as the men were lined up on the bridge and shot so that they fell into the canal. Ann's five men were hiding in the crawl space. Ann tried to shield her children so they would not see what was happening.

Ann and Willem had become very weak and thin from malnutrition. In December they decided to make a desperate trip the fifty miles to Enkhuizen to get some food. The children were given to the neighbors and the two set out for Enkhuizen by bicycle. The bikes were old and the tires were in horrible shape but they made it to the Kuiper house in Enkhuizen and obtained some rice powder, powdered milk and some other meager food items. Ann's mother scolded her for looking bad. On the way back to Delft the tires gave out several times and had to be patched.

"Ann and Willem toward the end of the war"

In 1876 the river "Y" was converted into the North Sea Canal. The dunes were breached to build a canal, dike and lock system that allowed large cargo ships into Amsterdam by avoiding the shallow Zuider Zee. The new North Sea entrance to the "Y" was named "mouth of the Y", or "Ymuiden". Willem and Ann had to go over a tall bridge at Ymuiden to get back to Delft. Ann was so tired that she asked Willem to rest before crossing the bridge. While they were resting, a British fighter plane machine gunned everything on the bridge. The fires on the bridge made the steel hot so that the tires on the bikes blew out while crossing the bridge and had to be patched again. Ann and Bill gratefully made it home to Delft.

The rice powder and powdered milk were emergency supplies for baby Willem. Ann was starving and no longer had milk to give. The beans that Willem was soaking to provide food were also gone. Willem built a bird trap consisting of a square of wire fencing on a wooden frame. The trap was propped up on one end and baited with some seed. If a bird landed under the trap, Willem would pull the string that pulled out the prop stick. Willem learned to clean sparrows for the soup. The end was coming.

In early winter next door neighbor Tony Brokx asked Willem if he had connections in Zeeland. Zeeland is a southern province of The Netherlands that was then already liberated by the Allied armies. Willem said, yes, he knew some farmers there. Tony suggested calling one of the Zeeland farmers to see if he could send some food. Willem laughed because the phone call would have to cross the German lines. Tony urged him to try anyway.

The call to Zeeland miraculously got through. The farmer Willem contacted would not believe at first that people were starving so close to his farm. He promised to send some food if possible and would try to do it right away. Willem gave the name of a friend's bakery in Delft that could receive it. Ten days later, a small cargo boat pulled up to the De Boo bakery on the "Hooikade", a boat dock in Delft. The bakery was a few doors from the Sluis Seed Company. The boat brought five very large sacks of potatoes. The De Boo family kept one and the other four were carefully hidden. The Sluis family was saved. The potatoes were shared with close friends.

In January a stranger came to the door with a leather shopping bag. A trusted friend had sent him to the Sluis household for some potatoes. He asked for some peels because his family was starving. Ann filled up the bag with potatoes although she knew that public knowledge of the food would probably result in the death of her family. The man left crying. He did not give the Sluis secret away and was not heard from again.

It was a very close call. In April, 1945, the Canadian Army liberated Delft. The Canadians were astounded at the emaciated people. Ann weighed 78 pounds. Willem weighed about 115 pounds. The children were barely alive. Riding on one of the Canadian tanks, a friend who Willem had known in Saint Remy-De-Provence recognized him. The friend, Retou, had made it out of France and had joined the Canadian Army. Willem called to him and he jumped from the tank, hugged Willem and asked him why he looked so awful. Willem explained the starvation and explained that he had a baby at home who was near death. That night, the Canadians delivered some rice powder to the Sluis home for starving baby Willem Jr. Ann credited the emergency delivery with saving her baby's life.

"The Canadians liberate Delft"

There was an emergency need for food for the whole region of Western Netherlands. The liberators tried to share food with the population but it was not enough. Supplies for the Canadian Army had to be brought by small roads from Antwerp in Belgium. The North Sea coast of Holland was still in enemy hands with heavy fortifications at the mouth of the Rhine and at Ymuiden which blocked ships and aircraft bringing needed supplies. Negotiation with the German defenders on the North Sea produced a truce that allowed relief flights by military planes to fly over the coastal forts at designated times and food deliveries by ship into Rotterdam. The event was announced by radio and in the newspapers.

On May 3, 1945 allied bombers flew over Delft again. This time they dropped food. The food was in cans, boxes and bags that were thrown out of the bomb bays to land in fields, in streets and in the city. The emergency was so great that there had been no time to prepare a better way. The people of Delft came outside of their homes. Willem and Ann with all three children stood on the roof tiles of the house to watch. The cans were badly dented, some items fell into canals, a few came through roofs, but most of the food survived. The Canadians quickly mobilized with help from the underground to gather all the food and arrange a fair distribution. The Sluis children tasted margarine for the first time. Many years later, Joost still remembered the brand: "Blue Band". White bread was a sensation!

"A bomber dropping food"

"Bags of food in the treeless fields"

"Food distribution"

The liberators brought food and sanitation. Delousing stations with DDT powder eliminated the lice and fleas. Soap reappeared along with running water. Military medical teams treated some of the sick in field hospitals and the city hospitals were restocked with supplies. Civilization started to return. Joost had rickets and would wear braces on his legs for over a year. Willem and Ann had lost all their teeth and would wear full dentures for the rest of their lives.

Surviving men who had already been freed from labor camps came home. A few weeks later, those who collaborated with the Germans were rounded up. The men were beaten or worse. Girls who had befriended the Germans had their heads shaved with sheep shearing tools, had green swastikas painted on their heads and were then run out of town. There was singing and dancing in the streets. The collaborators would later be tried in court. The war was over for Delft.

The churches of Delft held services of thanksgiving for deliverance from evil. Everyone went.

CHAPTER 5
AMERICA

The Germans had destroyed the center of Rotterdam but the other cities of The Netherlands had not been extensively bombed. Delft and Enkhuizen looked pretty much the way they looked before the war, without trees. The railroad stations, bridges and equipment were, however, badly damaged. Plans were made to replant all the missing trees. There were almost no trains, cars or boats. The country had no food, fuel, animals or consumer goods. Everyone was in rags.

Queen Wilhelmina and her court returned from England to a less than enthusiastic welcome. Many resented that she had fled.

Willem and Ann owned their house but Willem was unemployed. His money was almost gone. He made an attempt to restart the Sluis Seed business with the contacts he still had with seed growers and customers. Money was in short supply and competition was fierce. The project did not do well.

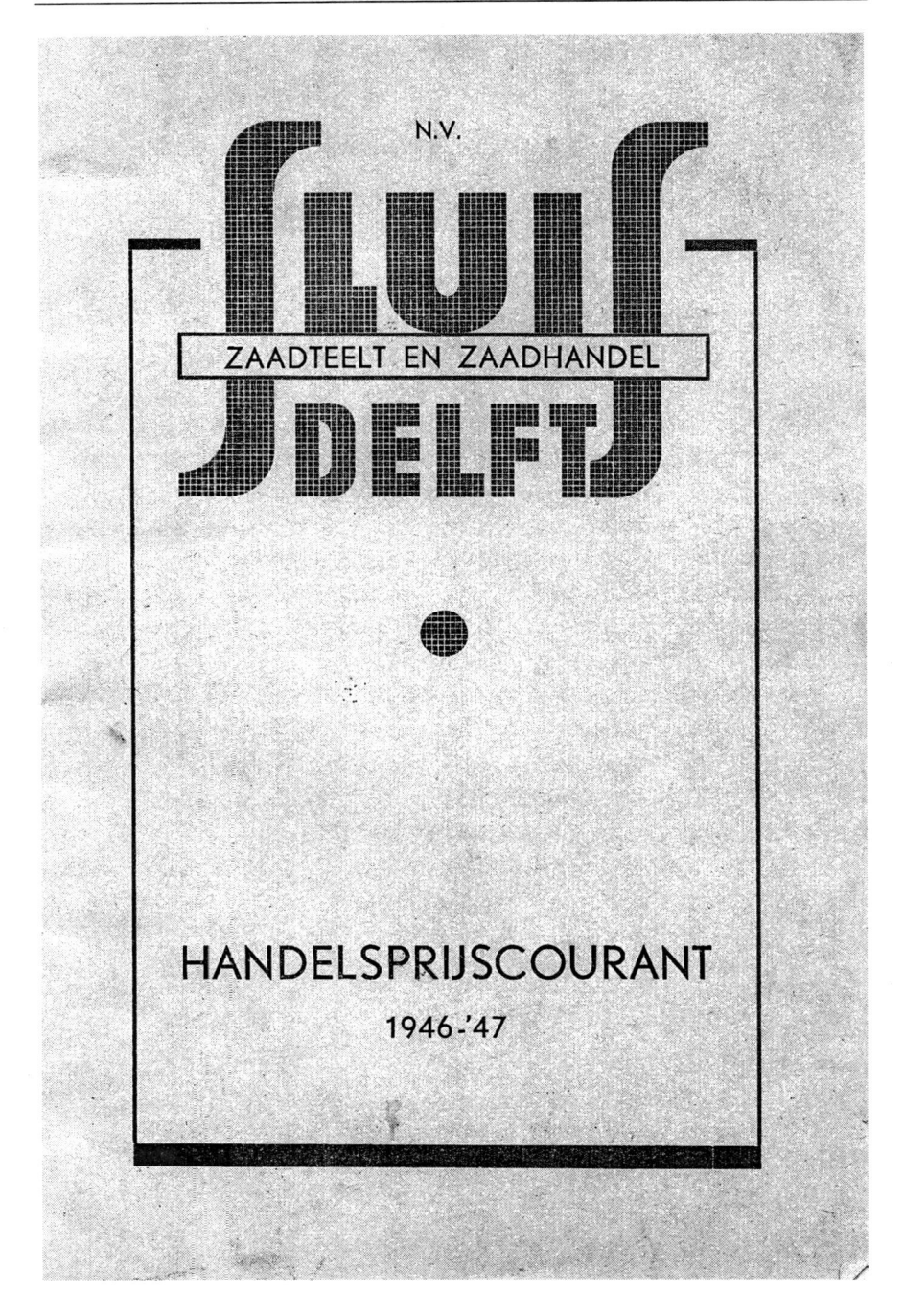

"1946 Catalog of the Sluis Seed Company"

After trying to restart the seed company Willem decided to return to work as a seed salesman and asked his father for a job selling seed. Jacob was a hard man and he refused to help. A competitor of Sluis Brothers gave Willem a job selling seed in the Soviet occupied countries of Eastern Europe. The seed needed to plant new crops had been destroyed or eaten in most of Europe along with all the livestock. Replacement seed to plant food crops was urgently needed. Willem traveled to Hungary and Poland and succeeded in selling seed to those countries. The Western Allies had placed an embargo on money transactions with Soviet occupied countries so that business transactions required a lot of ingenuity. Willem devised a scheme where the buyers delivered East German "Olympia" typewriters to an agent in Sweden who sold them for cash to pay for the seed. The sales job lasted a year or so. Willem and Ann still had their optimism and faith.

"Joost, Helen, Ann, Willem Jr. and Willem, in 1946"

The Americans flooded Western Europe with consumer goods. Ships from the Americas brought cattle and other livestock to restart meat and dairy production. The people of Delft were happy to have clothes and soap to buy again. The economy was very bad, but there was a slow beginning. The stores were open again, the people had food, the lights came on.

Bernard was born on August 9, 1946.

In the fall of 1946, Ann's brother in law, Aart Nauta, was called to active duty as a Sergeant in the Reserve of the Netherlands Army. He spent eighteen months in Indonesia fighting against rebels under Sukarno who were claiming independence from The Netherlands. Indonesia was part of The Kingdom of the Netherlands because of conquest by the East India Companies. The rebels ultimately won the war and Indonesia became independent.

On December 6, 1946 Saint Nicholas, known in The Netherlands as Sinterklaas, came to the Jewish home of the Brokx family next door to the Sluis home. The Brokx children, the Sluis children and other neighbors waited for his arrival. Sinterklaas is a gift to the children of Netherlands from the Spanish occupation. He arrives on a boat from Spain, rides a white horse and is accompanied by Moorish helpers. The children of Netherlands adore him and greatly fear what his helpers might do to them. On this Saint Nicholas Day, Sinterklaas arrived on his horse and entered the house. He had gifts for all the children and threw "peppernut" baked candies everywhere. His helpers, thankfully, did not give any of the children coal or, worse, stuff them into their bags and take them away. This was the first time that most of the children remembered seeing him. It was a memorable event.

"Saint Nicholas "Sinterklaas" comes to Delft"

In June of 1947, Father Jacob Sluis contacted Willem to tell him that Joost's body would be returned to The Netherlands from France for reburial in Enkhuizen. Willem, Ann and all the children traveled to Enkhuizen for the military reburial in the Sluis family plot.

Later in 1947, Willem decided that Europe was going to experience a slow recovery, offered few prospects for success and that he and his family should go the United States. He contacted the American Embassy in Amsterdam where he was told that his citizenship was revoked because he had voted in the Netherlands elections of 1946. Willem had to apply for reinstatement of his citizenship. He won and it was then established that he and his oldest son Joost were American citizens by birth but that the law was changed after Joost was born so that Helen, Willem Jr., and Bernard were Netherlands citizens with their mother.

In the spring of 1948, Willem found passage on a ship headed for the United States. He had relatives in Chicago and went there to start making a home for the family. The house in Delft was put up for sale. Ann and the four children stayed in Delft, where Ann sold a lot of her possessions to raise money. Her treasured piano had to be sold. The house sold in April of 1948 and Ann moved to Enkhuizen so she could spend her last few months in The Netherlands near her family and her mother. The remaining furniture was crated and stored for shipment to America.

An elderly neighbor lady brought a bible to Ann as a parting gift. She has heard of America and knew of Al Capone and the Indian wars. She thought that the Bible would be needed in the Godless country that the family was moving to.

Enkhuizen

Ann's father had found a small helper's house that could be rented on the farm of the Langedyk family on The Kruislaan in Enkhuizen. The house was a cottage on stilts made of green painted wood, without plumbing. The Langedyk farmstead was inside the city of Enkhuizen, a common occurrence in North Holland. Farmer Langedyk owned grazing and crop land in the polder outside the city and traveled there by flat bottomed boat to tend his cattle and crops. Several boats were normally tied up in the canal by the door of the farm. One boat was large enough to ferry a few cows at a time from one field to another or to and from the barn in the city. The farm house was an old fashioned Frisian house that consisted of a large barn with a house built into it on one end. The farm house was heated by a large tiled stove and cooking was done in the barn using a huge fireplace. The house Ann rented was a helper's cabin on the opposite end of the yard from the barn entrance.

The Sluis children had a wonderful time in Enkhuizen. They

made a lot of visits to "Oma" and "Opa" Kuiper. The greatest treat at the Kuiper house was being allowed to sleep in the enclosed antique bedstead in the attic that was built into the walls and had doors that closed. Grandpa Kuiper had chicken coops built along the wall at one side of the back yard that fascinated eight year old Joost and six year old Helen. Little four year old Willem Jr. tagged along. Ann was always in fear that her children would fall into one of the canals or the harbor.

Visits to the Jacob Sluis family home on the Westerstraat were a little more formal but also a lot of fun. The Sluis home was four stories tall and had lots of places to hide. There were also patio and a fish pond in the back yard with gold fish that Joost fell into at least once. The pond had a safety net of heavy fencing about one foot below the surface to make it safe.

Mr. and Mrs. Langedyk were friendly neighbors. Joost and Helen helped Mrs. Langedyk to make butter and cheese by being able to work the churn. They strained cheese curds through cheese cloth and learned about the cheese press. The attic of the farm house was a wonderful cheese loft with dozens of round cheeses aging in it. On one occasion, Mr. Langedyk permitted Joost to accompany him to the fields for a day in his boat.

On November 11, the children of Enkhuizen celebrated the Feast of St. Martin by going from door to door with paper lanterns on long sticks with candles in them. The children went to each door and sang in exchange for treats. This old Catholic tradition was not practiced in the parts of Holland that were "Dutch Reformed" but Enkhuizen still retained this celebration of St Martin of Tours. The farmers near Enkhuizen, including Mr. Langedyk, raised stock beets as winter fodder for their cattle. The beets were brought into the city by boat just before the cattle were brought in using the same boats and placed into the barns for the coldest weather. Stock beets are yellow, very large and wrinkled. As part of the St Martin celebration, particularly ugly looking beets were selected and hollowed out to make horrible faces that were then displayed. Some of them were hollowed out and had candles placed in them to shine through thin parts. Everyone competed to make the most gruesome face.

Chicago

In Chicago, Willem found helpful relatives and friends. His father's siblings Aafje, Dietje and Siebe lived in Chicago. Aafje was married to a mail man, a wonderful man named Joe Schneiders. Dietje was married to Cornelis Van Wyk. Willem's uncle Siebe lived behind his seed store on Halsted Street. There were also family members from the family of Willem's mother, one of whom, uncle Jacob "Jake" Sluis, owned the seed business begun by N. Sluis when he left the Sluis Seed Store. These relatives all helped Willem to get started.

Willem, now called William spoke good English but his educational credentials were not recognized. He ended up getting a job on the loading dock of the Continental Can Company on Western Avenue. When he had his job he rented a house and went to the federal court house in Chicago to fill out the paper work that would permit Ann to join him in the United States. Clerical errors ended up delaying approval of Ann's visa for four months.

Ann was anxious to rejoin her husband. The unexpected four months of delay in making the trip to New York was very difficult because her house was sold and money was in short supply. She tried to get passage to America but there was none to be had. She described her problem to father Jacob Sluis who then used his connections to get a cabin on the steam ship Nieuw Amsterdam of the Holland America Line. The ship sailed for New York on December 11, 1948 with all the brothers and sisters waving farewell from the dock in Rotterdam. Ann's remaining furniture was also shipped to Chicago.

"Relatives waving goodbye to Ann and her children"

"A huge storm at sea delayed the ship"

The Nieuw Amsterdam was used as a troop ship during the war and this was her first crossing since being refitted for passengers. The ship was beautifully outfitted. During the crossing, a huge Atlantic storm damaged the ship and delayed her arrival in New York until late in the day, in heavy snow, on December 20. Ann took the children up on deck and searched out the Statue of Liberty as the ship sailed by.

"The Statue of Liberty in the winter fog"

William and a friend, Al Doorn, were waiting dockside for the ship's arrival with Al's brand new automobile – a red Kaiser! The Kaiser automobile was a sensational new product at that time. It was manufactured by the world famous company of Henry J. Kaiser who had manufactured the "Victory Ships" of World War II. The company was now in the automobile business, using similar new highly advanced engineering and prefabrication techniques to those that had been used to produce ships in record times.

When the ship docked, all the Americans had to leave the ship first, followed by the immigrants. Ann spoke forcefully to the purser and arranged that her son Joost would be the last American to leave the ship and that she would be the first immigrant. Everyone piled into the large new car and headed for the Statler Hotel in New York.

The next morning, the whole group went downstairs to eat breakfast. William insisted that the children be given American foods such as pork and beans and pancakes. The children had never tasted American food before and could not eat it. The unfamiliar sweet taste of corn permeated all the food and made it distasteful to them. After breakfast, all piled into the Kaiser and headed for Chicago, packed in and happy. Friend Al had selected a brand new highway for the trip – advertised as one of the wonders of the world because it had been built through mountains. The Pennsylvania Turnpike had just opened and was a sensation. The weather was very cold and snowy.

The arrival in Chicago was just before Christmas. Everyone went to Al's house. Al had a television set – none of the Hollanders had seen one yet. It was decided to split up the family among relatives while William looked for a place to live. The children were spoiled at Christmas and lavished with attention. There were skates and sleds, new clothes and shoes, it was a wonderful Christmas. The Netherlands does not get much snow so that the amount of snow in Chicago was a big surprise to the children.

"Joost and Helen with the new sled in the Chicago snow"

William, now called Bill, and Ann had found a place to live for the family at 6523 South May Street. It was a filthy house located on the alley where a garage would normally go behind the main house. The land lady, a Mrs. Friel, gave permission to fix up the place so Bill and Ann signed a one year lease and went to work. Everything was cleaned, new wallpaper and linoleum flooring were put in and the house was turned into a suitable home. The crate of furniture from Delft was unpacked. The children moved in to reunite the family in mid January, 1949. Joost helped by bringing in buckets of coal for the stove.

Ann enrolled the older children in the Chicago Public School located in Ogden Park on Racine Street about a block away. She went to the school to observe and was dismayed by what she saw, the children were promptly removed from the Public School to be enrolled at the Englewood Christian School on 71st Street. The family attended the First Christian Reformed Church with all the aunts, uncles and friends.

Bill and Ann spoke English but the children did not. Joost was in the third grade in The Netherlands but was now placed back into the first grade. He was given the first grade readers and helped to catch up to his peers. Joost was promoted every six months until he caught up with his age group at fifth grade. Helen caught up to be in the fourth grade after a similar regimen.

The family was adapting to America. Everyone would walk the quarter mile to the nearest supermarket – the HI-LO store on 63rd Street. Ann had bought a "HI-LO Flyer" coaster wagon that was used to haul the little kids and the groceries. On one memorable day, the whole family was in the HI-LO when Ann called across the store: "Pa, you want a kissie"? The others shoppers took note. What no one else knew was that Ann was asking Bill if he wanted a wooden box of Velveeta Cheese. In the Netherlands language, a small crate is a "Kistje", pronounced in slang as "kissie", and Velveeta came in a wooden box in those days.

Bill and Ann celebrated their tenth wedding anniversary on May 16, 1949. They and their four children were healthy and they looked forward to the future with confidence. Bill started looking into business opportunities. He was working at odd jobs in those days, including a period of working for his friend Al Doorn who was a concrete contractor. The work for Al was physically too hard for Bill and did not last long. A similar job for a cousin in the industrial trash business was also a short one.

"Christmas 1949"

When the time came to renew the lease on the house in early 1950, Mrs. Friel surprised Bill and Ann by doubling the rent because the house had been greatly improved. Bill got mad and refused to sign. Uncle Siebe came to the rescue by permitting the family to move to the apartment above his seed store at 7219 South Halsted Street. The apartment was empty and had been used for storage.

Above the seed store, history repeated itself through Bill and Ann who cleaned the apartment, wallpapered and painted it to make it into a nice home. The apartment had a street entrance next to the store with a tall stairway going upstairs. After the family had moved in, Bill spent several days standing on a ladder carefully painting gray lines on the transom window above the street door to make it look like glass and lead. In the middle of the glass and lead pattern, he placed the Sluis family crest. It was a work of art.

It was while living on Halsted Street that the Sluis children learned to like television. Their first television set at Al Doorn's house had always been switched to football when they saw it which made no sense to them. Now a neighbor boy named "Skippy" invited Joost and Helen to come to his house one Saturday morning to watch "Flash Gordon". They loved it and would beg every Saturday to watch. Everything went very well for a while until Joost and Skippy decided to scare Skippy's mother. The basement of their house had clothes lines for winter drying that the two ten year old boys equipped with false ghosts made of bed sheets. When Skippy's mother came down stairs one day, the boys pulled on the clothes lines, which were on pulleys, and the ghosts moved rapidly toward the stairs in the dark basement. "Flash Gordon" became harder to arrange.

John Paul was born on June 11, 1950.

At the end of 1950, Uncle Siebe's wife Tina decided that Bill and Ann would have to move from the upstairs apartment because she now wanted it. Bill and Ann started looking again. Renting an apartment with five children was almost impossible in 1950 Chicago. There were no rent laws that compelled landlords to rent to families and very few would. Finding a new place to live proved to be difficult.

CHAPTER 6
SUNNY ACRES

The Sluis Brothers seed company in Enkhuizen owned five acres of land located at the corner of 95th Street and Western Avenue in Evergreen Park, Illinois that had been used by the Sluis Seed Store to raise onion seed in the early 1900's. In the early spring of 1950, Bill received permission to plant the field with a crop. He and son Joost plowed the five acres with a garden tiller and Bill then planted witlof, a Belgian specialty endive vegetable. Bill expected that the endive would bring a high price in the community of former Hollanders, as it did in Europe. He had not reckoned with Chicago tastes – the large Dutch community in Chicago no longer looked for the vegetable. The project did not succeed. The company sold land the following year to a developer for the "Evergreen Shopping Center".

That fall, Bill was still looking for an apartment to rent when a friend told him that some war veterans were building their own homes. Bill was amazed that such a thing could be done in the United States. The Netherlands government had taken such rights from the people long ago through regulations and rules. He and Ann found out that the United States had freedom far beyond their European expectations. Blueprints could be purchased from "Better Homes and Gardens" magazine and other sources to permit "do it yourself" construction. Bill and Ann decided to try since renting had been a very bad experience.

They started looking for a place to build and bought an old Oldsmobile car to search with. After about a month they found a subdivision called "Sunny Acres" located next to a little farm town named Mokena. The town was 32 miles from Chicago which was very far from the city but the soil looked good and the price was affordable. Two lots were purchased that were 100 feet wide and 300 feet deep on 192nd Street in a subdivision called "Sunny Acres" for $1150 – less than $1,000 per acre. Bill and Ann were able to pay for the lots with money sent by Ann's father Bernard Kuiper.

The magazine "Better Homes and Gardens" of 1950 was full of do it yourself ideas for home building and gardening. A book, "Five Acres and Independence" by M. G. Kevins, described in great detail how a small farm could be the source of an idyllic family life. The book described how a family could live handsomely by raising everything needed on a five acre plot of land. The magazine and book became the source of Bill's new dreams for the future. A set of blueprints and a home construction manual were bought from the magazine to start working on the dream.

A farmer named Marion Owens who lived south of the town was a student of anthropology. He made regular trips to the University of Illinois where he contributed his findings and collaborated with the anthropology staff. His discovery was that the native roads that connected the area near what is now Detroit, Michigan with the Mississippi river met near his farm, which was full of native artifacts. US Highway 30 lies about three miles south of Mokena and roughly connects the ancient Sauk Trail from Michigan with the Blackhawk Trail from Southwestern Wisconsin. The two ancient roads met near the bank of Hickory Creek between US 30 and the land that would become Mokena. Native nations met annually and elected a Great Chief over all the people. Mud Turtle was the last such chief, and his name, Mokena, was given to the town.

The Germans who settled the land found that the heavy soil did not drain well enough for crops. They partly cleared it for pasture and created a dairy cooperative. The cooperative built a milk storage house about two miles east of the town on the banks of Hickory Creek. Ice cut from the creek in winter kept the milk fresh until the train came to pick it up for Chicago sale. The Rock Island railroad made two stops per week to pick up milk at Mokena and the Nickel Plate railroad made two stops per week in Frankfort about two miles South of the milk house. The dairy economy supported the town until the Great Depression.

During Prohibition, a large dance hall flourished just south of the town in "Woodland Circle" that drew large crowds of partiers and drinkers from Chicago by train. The largest business in town, a brewery on Wolf Road at the railroad tracks was converted to the Bowman Dairy, then to a wallpaper mill. Mokena once had a high school but tore it down when the economy declined in the 1930's. The town stayed small with about six hundred persons in 1950. Three churches were located on a square in the center of town – two Lutheran and one Presbyterian – and a small Catholic church was tolerated just outside the town boundaries on the north side. German families with names like Yunker and Hostert ruled. The townspeople were clannish and unaccustomed to strangers. Front Street ran along the tracks.

In 1951 the town was reached by roads through corn fields and pastures. Wolf Road, the main road through town had little traffic. The big milk house was no longer used because mechanical refrigeration had taken over. Some farm fields had been improved with drainage systems that would permit corn to grow. There was a grain elevator near the train station that did a reasonable amount of business. The dairy business slowly declined. Front Street was slowly fading as more people started buying automobiles and going to other places to shop instead of walking to the stores. It was a little farm town like thousands of others in America. Very few people in Chicago had ever heard of it.

Do it yourself house building was traditional in the United States and was still common in 1951. The older roads of the United States are lined with houses that were built by returning veterans and others after World War II. Many have a homemade look about them, but all are monuments to the courage and perseverance of the families that built them. They were usually constructed in stages with banks lending money in installments for the projects. If the land was paid for then enough money would be lent for the basic shell of the house. If the shell was complete then enough would be lent to finish the project.

Aunt Tina had agreed to wait with her move into the Halsted Street apartment until the house in Mokena was ready. The project began in the early spring of 1951. Bill and Ann obtained a loan for initial construction and started.

The hole dug for the basement looked huge and was wet with standing water. Bill worked in the mud to make forms for the foundation footing of the house and the footing was poured. A large load of cement blocks was delivered and Bill and Ann started learning how to build a block wall with mortar. Bill had done light work in the fields of the seed company when young but Ann had never done hard physical work. Ten year old Joost carried the cement blocks to Ann and Bill as they laid the blocks and mixed the mortar by hand. Little baby John was on a blanket near the Kool Aid cooler and the coffee pot. John was tied to a stake with a rope because of fear that he would crawl to the foundation hole and fall in. Daughter Helen was mother to the smaller children while Ann worked with Bill. Willem Junior (Bill Jr.) and Bernard (Ben) played. The basement wall took almost two months.

"The family Oldsmobile with baby John on his blanket and tied to a rope"

"Building the basement wall in the mud"

During construction of the basement, a coal chute was needed. A coal chute was a steel door that a truck could use to unload coal directly into the basement. Bill bought the chute from Montgomery Ward in Chicago and left Joost at home one day so he could take the street car down Halsted Street to pick it up. The Montgomery Ward warehouse was about ten miles North near Halsted Street, just across the Chicago River on Chicago Avenue. Joost took the street car to Chicago Avenue and crossed the bridge to Montgomery Ward. He picked up the coal chute and found that he could barely lift it. He made it back to Halsted Street by lifting and carrying it ten feet at a time. A stranger helped him put it onto the street car. Joost came home exhausted.

The family made almost daily trips to Mokena. The trip took an hour each way, traveling on the "Southwest Highway" out of Chicago. Everyone got up early. The work on the house progressed all summer. On rainy days the family stayed in Chicago. The house framing was a lot more work than either Bill or Ann had realized but they continued bravely on. Ann and Bill worked together to build their house. Both of them learned how to climb ladders cut wood and do carpentry by trial and error. Helpful lumber yard workers readily gave advice. By September, the roof was going on.

All sawing and drilling had to be done by hand. There was no electricity on the building site and electric hand tools were an expensive rarity in those days. The house was sheathed in boards and roofed with similar boards. The sheathing was covered with tar paper that was held in place with numerous wooden furring strips. The roof was tar paper and asphalt shingles. Bill and Ann carried it all up the ladders together.

"The roof rafters are started"

"Joost and Ann nailing a roof board"

78 · COMING TO MOKENA

"Bill and Ann as carpenters"

In the spring of 1951, Bill's father Jacob came to the United States and visited his brother Siebe in Chicago. One rainy day Joost saw his grandfather on the Halsted Street sidewalk below the apartment window, called everyone to the window to see "Opa", and asked to go downstairs to greet him. Bill would not permit the children to go downstairs. The enmity between the two men now became clear. The children did not see their grandfather again.

In the fall the older children were enrolled in the Mokena Elementary School on Carpenter Street. The principal, Mrs. Elizabeth Kappel, was dubious about the grade level but Bill convinced her that the parents were supportive and that the new strangers would do well. Joost, Helen and Bill Jr. were now dropped off at the school in the morning while Ann, Bill and the two small ones continued camping at the construction site.

Aunt Tina was getting restless. She had not expected to wait until the end of 1951 to move to the upstairs apartment. She finally put her foot down – Bill and Ann moved their family into the unfinished house.

The William Sluis family moved into a barely functional house in the late fall of 1951. The house was covered with tar paper on the outside. There were no interior walls. The stairs going up consisted of a hand made wooden ladder. Ann was in constant fear that one of the children would fall. The floors were bare boards. The basement had no floor and was filled with water. There was no plumbing or electric service. The front and back doors were nailed together out of boards. Bill had constructed a homemade furnace for the house made of two 55 gallon oil drums using a magazine design, but it did not work.

The house was in the "Cape Cod" style with a steep roof that had a second floor under it. The first winter the family lived on the second floor. Bill and Ann had insulated the East end of the floor. A small "Warm Morning" coal stove was placed there with a temporary stove pipe going out through a window to heat the space. A blanket was hung to isolate the heated part from the other half of the second floor. The neighbors behind the house provided electricity through a 500 foot long piece of "Romex" cable that powered a couple of light bulbs. The toilet was a chamber pot on the first floor. Water was carried by bucket from an outside faucet of the house across the street. Conditions were barely better than those in Delft of 1945. The whole family slept in two large beds to keep warm.

"The house in the winter of 1951 – with
the stove pipe from the second floor stove"

There was no refrigerator or kitchen and food was basic. The milk for the family was evaporated, canned milk, which everyone learned to drink mixed half and half with water. Canned goods were purchased by the case to save money. The diet was based on potatoes, vegetables and grain with some meat. Everything was cooked on the "Warm Morning" stove. The family had not learned to eat foods that do not grow in Northern Europe such as squash, eggplant, green peppers or corn. Simple American foods such as pop corn were unknown and smelled funny. The milk on the table would sometimes freeze when the coal stove got too cool in the middle of the night. Ann would cook a warm breakfast of oat meal or "Farina" and send the three oldest children off to school in the town, 1 ½ miles away.

Bill and Ann were loyal Christians. In Mokena, they had to face the fact that the nearest Christian Reformed church was almost an hour's drive away in good weather and that this meant that their children would not be taught the faith in a proper school. They started shopping for a church in Mokena by interviewing the pastors concerning doctrine and church disciplines. Pastor Gode of the Immanuel Lutheran Church was their eventual choice and the entire family was conditionally baptized again as Missouri Lutheran. It would prove to be a good choice. The family regularly attended church and all the children were eventually confirmed as Lutheran.

The Sluis family was a mystery to the six hundred people of Mokena. The children were neatly dressed, well behaved, very healthy and had a strange accent. Foreigners were almost unknown in little Mokena and people talked. Most were complimentary about the way that Bill and Ann raised their kids.

"Bill Jr., Helen, Ben, Joost, John and Ann, winter 1951"

The crude housing arrangement on 192nd Street slowly became public knowledge. It came to the attention of a teacher named Marcella Lehmann who lived in Mokena. Marcella came to Ann and proposed that Ann and her babies might enjoy being in a warm house every school day. Ann became the house keeper for Marcella, riding her bicycle to town, fixing lunches for the Sluis and Lehmann children and cleaning while caring for baby John and little Ben. The house was directly across the street from the elementary school on Carpenter Street. Bill went to work at the

R.O.W. Window Company in Rockdale.

Entertainment at night came from a large console radio that Bill had gotten from his cousin Norman. The radio was the center of the household with the children sitting on the floor in front of it listening to "The Shadow" and "Luigie Basco, the Little Immigrant", which were the favorite programs. Bill listened to the news, "Amos and Andy" and traditional classical music. Ann liked to listen to the Christian broadcast of the Moody Bible Institute on WMBI Radio as well as the classics. The children continued to improve their English, partly because father Bill had forbidden the speaking of the Netherlands language in the house so the children would not grow up with accented speech.

While Bill and Ann were building in 1951, a Polish American family named Jasinski bought a building lot across the street. Their oldest daughter, Susan, decided then that Ann Sluis was the meanest mother in the world because she kept her baby tied up to a rope. She did not accept the rationale until many years later. The Jasinskis started building their house in the spring of 1952.

The Sluis house improved a lot in 1952. Money was found to have a concrete floor put into the basement. Bill found a used "Holland" coal fired furnace and installed it in the basement together with large air ducts to heat the house. It took him almost two months to build the 32 foot tall house chimney out of brick from the basement floor to two feet above the ridge of the house. Insulation was finished in the entire house and some interior walls had wall board. The stairs was put in to both the basement and the upstairs. The house now had electric service. There was still no water or plumbing but improvement was dramatic. The house was now heated, insulated and had many fewer drafts. The wooden siding was installed on the outside of the house although the front porch and back porch were still temporary. Ann and Bill were still full of enthusiasm but the hard life was taking a toll on Bill, who began taking refuge in wine occasionally.

Joost and Helen met the Dina children who lived a block South. The Dinas had a television set and sometimes hosted the Sluis children. The houses in Sunny Acres were far apart which limited the number of nearby playmates. The Sluis and Jasinski children became close while their new house was being built across the street. Joost began delivering newspapers by bicycle daily.

The Jasinski house progressed so that at the end of 1952 their basement had been turned into a temporary house. "Renie" Jasinski had better analyzed the work involved so that he had his temporary house somewhat more ready that the Sluis house of 1951 had been. In the 1950's many of the house plans available for do it yourself builders included ideas such as building the garage first to use as a temporary home during construction of the main house. The Jasinski plan was not extreme for the time. Electricity was sent to the Jasinski house by means of a long cable from the Sluis house that crossed the street by being raised on the top of a fourteen foot board.

Bill sent away for plans and a kit to build his own table saw. He laboriously cut and drilled plywood by hand and made a splendid machine that would tilt and control depth. An electric motor powered it. Homeowners rarely had power tools in those days and generally built them as Bill was doing. Factory made table saws were commercial units and very expensive. The saw was built because Bill planned a plant business and wanted to make wooden planting boxes or "flats" for seeds and seedlings. He bought a large number of used shipping crates from oranges cheaply and made a lot of flats. The basement also still had a large pile of orange crates

At the end of 1952 two more lots were purchased so that Bill and Ann owned four lots of land for a total property of 400 feet by 300 feet.

During the winter of 1952 it turned out that the Jasinski basement leaked when it rained. On some nights, the five Jasinskis: Renie, his wife Adeline and their children Tom, Susan and Christine would cross the street and sleep on the first floor of the Sluis residence. The door was always unlocked.

Bill bought a used International panel truck in early 1953. The Oldsmobile had given out. In the 1950's all trucks were considered commercial vehicles and Illinois law required that the name of the owner had to be painted on the doors. The Sluis panel truck - in later years it would have been called a van - with the name Wm. Sluis painted on the side was a fixture in Mokena for many years. The truck was painted two tone green with a paint brush and had the name painted on the doors in yellow. Since the panel truck had only one seat, a chair was placed on the left side for Ann. The chair was from the original deluxe furnishings at Ons Genoegen but now the broken chair arms had been sawed off and it was old and utilitarian. The panel truck became a family treasure. Orange crates were placed behind Bill and Ann for the kids to sit on. The truck took them to church, shopping, and most wonderfully to the Hill Top Drive In movie in Joliet where the family enjoyed some happy times. The little kids would sleep in the back of the truck on blankets when they became tired while the rest of the family enjoyed the movies.

In the spring of 1953, Bill sent to a farm in Texas for thousands of rooted tomato plants from cuttings. A local farmer plowed two of the four lots in Sunny Acres and Bill with his son Joost prepared the soil with the garden tiller. The entire family planted 1 ½ acres of tomatoes at the beginning of May. Bill, Ann and Joost planted, Helen brought Kool Aid to drink and took care of the smaller children. A large part of that spring and summer was spent cultivating the tomatoes with the result that a wonderful harvest was achieved. The tomatoes were the first harvest that reached the Chicago Randolph Street market that year. Bill was paid $28 per basket for the first delivery with slowly decreasing prices later. Bill made the first trip alone but let Joost come with him on the second. The two left Mokena at 4 AM and arrived at about 5. A very strong cup of coffee in a corner diner was part of the plan. After selling the tomatoes, Bill and Joost visited the N. Sluis and Son Seed Company on Randolph Street that was owned by Bill's uncle "Jake" Sluis. The tomato growing business was a great success that would have been even greater had it been possible to bring all of the tomatoes to the market when prices dropped later in the season.

"The panel truck, Helen modeling, in front of the tomato field"

The family needed more income, so Ann obtained a job at the American Institute of Laundering in Joliet, a large commercial laundry. The work there was too hard for her so she quit after a few weeks. Later in the year she was hired at the Gould Company in Rockdale which manufactured slip covers. Bill still worked for the R.O.W. Window Company so that Ann and Bill went to work together in the panel truck.

In 1954 a well was dug and water became available in the house. There was no inside piping yet but a garden hose that was hooked to the pump in the basement made water more convenient. More work was done on interior walls and some plywood flooring was laid. Joost graduated from the Mokena Elementary School. Bill built a chicken house and a chick brooder that was heated by a light bulb. Fifty baby chicks arrived in the spring. When the chicks were large enough, the roosters were selected for the cooking pot two at a time and the hens were allowed to stay in the chicken house. The family now ate a lot of eggs. A refrigerator and kitchen stove appeared. Bottled milk was bought from the Shiek Dairy at the end of the street. Ann was able to bring a lot of cloth scraps home from the slipcover factory that she used to make covers for her aging furniture. The family was happy but poor since all available cash still went into the house.

American dry breakfast cereal made its appearance in the Sluis house. The cereal of choice was "Nabisco Shredded Wheat", which was adopted as the standard. The shredded wheat was popular primarily because it came in boxes that had cardboard dividers between the biscuits. The divider cardboards were printed with wonderful projects such as model airplanes and other wonders that could be built from them. When a new box of shredded wheat came home, the older Sluis kids would fight over the divider boards and would take all the biscuits out of the box to get them. Ann would not permit throwing away the biscuits, which were eaten after soaking in milk for half an hour to make them more like oatmeal.

Ann obtained a clerical job in the "Insurance Exchange" in downtown Chicago. Her 1931 diploma from business school and recommendations from Mokena acquaintances landed her the job. In the meantime, Bill had changed jobs and was working for a large Chicago florist, "Amling's Flower Land" on North Avenue. Commuting to Chicago using the Rock Island Railroad was expensive so Ann would often ride with Bill to North Avenue where she could take cheaper transportation to downtown. Both Bill and Ann now had work more suited to their temperaments but their days were very long. Joost and Helen ran the household in the daytime and each of the Sluis kids was assigned work to do in a "Pecking order". Potato peeling, dish washing, dish drying, chicken feeding and other jobs became institutionalized. Ann usually came home with meat for dinner from Wannamaker's IGA Store on Front Street in Mokena. The meat was ordered the day before and picked up when Ann came home. The Sluis children would have the rest of the meal ready to cook. The house was not finished enough to have friends visit so that play with children other than the Jasinskis was confined to the school yard. Joost started to do work to finish the house.

Mokena had an annual carnival known as the "Mokena Homecoming". This event was held on the last weekend of August in the railroad parking lot on Front Street. A carnival company would come and set up the Ferris wheel, the tilt-a-whirl and other rides.

Carnival booths would appear and various civic organizations would involve themselves with the planning. Ann was riding the train home from work on the Friday of the Homecoming when someone told her that "The DP's won the Chinchillas". In those days, there were a lot of news reports about displaced persons from World War II who had to be relocated from camps in Europe and Asia. The term DP, meaning "displaced person" was in the language. Ann did not know that the good citizens of Mokena were calling the Sluis family "DP's" and was deeply offended.

The Mokena Homecoming had an annual raffle. The big prize in 1954 was a set of mating chinchillas with a cage, a month's supply of feed and other items. It turned out that Bill Sluis was the winner! The prize was advertised as a sure way to riches since the chinchillas would breed like the rats they were and bring huge profits in the fur trade. The chinchillas were duly installed in the Sluis basement where they produced two young. During the winter, unfortunately, all of them died. The basement had not been provided with drain pipes around the perimeter and was always wet so that it was too damp for the animals.

In the fall of 1954, Joost was in the first Freshman Class at Lincoln-Way High School. Helen started the eighth grade in the Mokena Elementary School. The family was established in Mokena.

That same fall the family went to the Brookfield Zoo. Outings were not very common so it was a great event. Everyone piled into the panel truck for the hour's drive. It was a beautiful day with the older children enthralled by the animals and little Johnny riding high atop his father's neck. During the afternoon the family came to a large outdoor cage of monkeys. Two of the monkeys were having sex and a large crowd was watching. Suddenly, little four year old John Sluis yelled out "Ride 'em cowboy", and brought the house down.

CHAPTER 7
MOKENA

1955 was the year of the plumbing. The Sluis house needed a septic system for its waste disposal. Bill dug a huge hole on the East side of the house and built a 10,000 gallon tank of cement blocks. It was almost an underground house with a cement floor. While building the wooden form for the concrete roof, Bill fell into the tank and hurt his back badly. He wore a back brace for most of the summer that year. Even with his back brace, he and Joost installed black iron soil pipes in the house and galvanized drain pipes for the bathtub and kitchen sink. A toilet and bathtub were installed in the bathroom. A deep sink was installed in the basement for the washing machine.

Kitchen cabinet kits were purchased from Sears and Ann varnished all the cabinets and doors. The kitchen and bathroom were ready for water.

Bill bought copper pipe and flaring equipment and installed the water pipes. An electric water heater was installed in the basement. The copper piping leaked badly and was later replaced by son Joost with galvanized pipe. The house had plumbing!

Helen graduated from the Mokena Elementary School and started at Lincoln Way High School.

The old "Holland" furnace in the basement was manually stoked with coal. Bill had spent the winters since 1952 going down to the basement several times each night to put more coal into the fire box. The heat had sometimes been pretty uneven. In the summer of 1955 he found a used automatic stoker and installed it. The stoker worked with a screw mechanism to slowly push coal into the furnace to keep it burning steadily. A knob controlled the speed of the electric machine. The big hopper on the machine had to be filled once a day with coal. It was wonderful and Bill could now sleep through the night in the winter.

In the fall of 1955 construction of the greenhouse began. Bill had been planning this step for a long time and went to Wisconsin with a rented truck to pick up a large load of used steel pipe for the heating system. He worked very hard to build the greenhouse, to treat everything with wood preservative and to cover the buildings with plastic. Joost helped when he could. A shed was attached to the greenhouse on the west end that was equipped with a boiler for the heating system. It took several cold months to get all the pipes in place. They were arranged like one continuous radiator along the outside walls. Greenhouse benches were built out of treated one inch boards. The outside of the house was covered with a brand new type of plastic that had just become available. By March of 1956 all was ready.

"The Bill Sluis greenhouse"

Bill planted thousands of seeds for annual plants. He saw that the suburban life style created a large market for annuals such as flowers and easy to grow vegetables. His business was the first in Illinois to cater to the new need. The flats he had made from orange crates with the table saw were now filled with soil that he sterilized using steam from the boiler. By early May several hundred flats of annuals were ready to market.

"Bill in his greenhouse"

Joost built six large shelving units that could be used to display the plants at local stores. The shelves came apart for transport and were painted green. The Sears, Roebuck store in Joliet agreed to sell the plants for Bill on a consignment basis. All looked good until it turned out that the employees of the Sears store would not water the thirsty plants. The manager of the Sears store would not provide the labor for the job. It proved to be impossible to make two and three trips per day to care for the plants.

Mrs. Marge Bernardin had a flower shop in Mokena. Bill was able to place some of his plants at her store for sale and found that sales were slow. It was possible to water them at the Bernardin store, however. Bill operated the greenhouse for three spring seasons. Each year different stores would carry plants and Bill would stock the shelves and replenish them. Other plants such as geraniums sold well. The business did not make much profit but it proved the concept. Bill's knowledge and vision turned out to be right on target. Other entrepreneurs would later have great success in the enterprise that Bill pioneered.

The kitchen table was home to a wonderful chromed toaster. The toaster became a celebrity in the household because one morning the four boys caught teen aged Helen admiring herself in its mirror like surface. Helen could hold her own with her brothers but they now made her life miserable by christening her "Miss Toaster", a teasing name that would be used off and on for the next several years. Helen secretly knew that her brothers admired her looks but had to defend herself.

Bill and Ann were still working at Amling's and The Insurance Exchange when a man approached Ann on the train one day to ask if she might like to work for the railroad. Ann had impressed him and some of his friends with her pleasant and friendly demeanor and attractive dress. Working for the railroad was almost everyone's desire in Mokena since railroad workers had a pass to ride the trains for free. The gentleman's name was Needham and he arranged for an interview for Ann. She was hired by the Chicago, Rock Island and Pacific Railroad Company. Her 1931 business diploma was instrumental in the hire. She went to work in the company payroll department.

The Mokena Homecoming was sponsored by the Chamber of Commerce and the Lions Club. In 1956 a disaster struck that permanently erased enthusiasm for the project. On the last Saturday night of August, while the carnival was in full swing, a thunderstorm struck with ferocious winds that may have been a tornado. The Ferris wheel was wrecked. Power lines came crashing down. The whole town went dark. Joost and a girl friend were stuck on the Tilt-a-Whirl for almost an hour, in pouring rain, because live power lines were lying on the ride. Helen and Bill Jr. were sheltering in a store. Ann came rushing to town to see what happened to her children. No one was seriously hurt but there were no more Mokena Homecomings. There was a lot of costly damage to the town and to the equipment.

As a Christmas present in 1956 Ann bought a Sears "Silvertone" portable television set for the family. She paid for it by making contract payments of $5 per month. The TV was a thrilling thing for all and everyone wanted to watch his favorite shows. Bill and Ann strictly controlled watching time, however. The family would all watch together and see shows such as "I Love Lucy" and Bill's favorite "The Jackie Gleason Show".

The Sluis house continued to slowly improve. Natural gas came to Mokena and the old "Holland" coal furnace and the stoker went to the junk pile to be replaced by a new forced air gas heating system. Joost ripped out the coal chute and replaced it with a window. The rooms now all had wall board in them. Most of the interior trim boards were in place. The house had legitimate doors inside and out. It was a house although there were still incomplete elements here and there. The family still did not socialize. The children had friends at school but very few contacts of any kind. Joost had a girl friend, Bonnie, who had been arranged by his sister. He knew nothing of sports. The Sluis family had lived a hermit like existence for many years that was now beginning to end.

By 1958 the house was reasonably complete. In August, Bill and Ann decided to make a trip to The Netherlands to visit the family and report on ten years in America. Joost was eighteen years old and Helen was sixteen, so the two oldest children were left in charge of the house and family.

"Bill and Ann on board the SS United States
on their way home to Enkhuizen"

The family car at that time was a 1956 Ford station wagon – the panel truck was semi retired. Joost and Helen both drove the car. Helen had a boy friend at the time named Don who lived in Indiana and who attended Purdue University in Lafayette. She wanted to see her friend Don badly so Joost,18; Helen,16; Bill,14; Ben,12 and John,8 all went to Lafayette together. The trip was about 100 miles on US Highway 52. When the family was 26 miles from its goal of Lafayette, the car's gasoline tank fell off, carrying a piece of the frame and the brake lines with it. Joost was driving, and he ditched the car. No one was hurt but they were stuck in Indiana on a Friday night.

A passing motorist went to the nearest garage and sent help back. The five youngsters rode to the town in the tow truck and a repair was discussed. The mechanic stated that he could solder the gas tank, weld the frame back together and fix the brakes for a total price of $70. It had to be done. Helen called her boy friend and he came to pick everyone up and take them to Lafayette.

The five youngsters rented two rooms at a hotel in Lafayette and Helen was able to go out with her beloved Don. The family was divided with Joost, Bill and Ben in one room and Helen and John in the other. The hotel detective did not trust this arrangement and checked up on the group often that night.

Joost borrowed a bicycle and rode back on Saturday night to pick up the Ford. The mechanic was as good as his word and the car was ready. The group went back home on Sunday, having spent almost all the money that Bill and Ann had left behind.

Thirty years later, Helen confessed that the weekend before Ann and Bill left she had fallen asleep at the wheel in Northern Indiana while driving home in the Ford from a date with Don. She had flown off the road and landed in a deep depression at high speed. Ford Motor Company was vindicated.

Joost decided that he would dry up the perpetually damp basement while Bill and Ann were gone and dug all around the house to install drain pipes outside the house foundation that ended up in the sump for the house pump. Digging was relatively easy because the house, like most of the houses being built at that time, had been backfilled with slag from the steel mills. Slag is a foamy glass that comes from steel refining and it was preferred over soil because it acted like sand and would not settle over time. The basement project was a success.

When Bill and Ann came back from The Netherlands, they were angry and happy at the same time. Their trip had been a wonderful success. At home they were happy because the children survived and angry at what seemed to be high risk taking with both the car trip and the foundation dig. Ann was especially upset that the rose bushes she had planted on the East side of the house were killed during the digging.

Bill and Ann celebrated their twentieth wedding anniversary on May 19, 1959

Their marriage was sound and their mutual love and support had carried them through great tests of their strength. They had also become respected citizens of Mokena.

"Bill and Ann's house in 1960"

In 1959, Bill decided to try another business, this time the construction of a house for profit. The Sluis house was on the Westernmost lot of the four owned in Sunny Acres, now a new house was to be constructed on the most Eastern lot. A modern set of blueprints was obtained at no charge from New Lenox Lumber and Hardware. Construction began in early 1960.

Joost had been in and out of schools without much success. He was home in the spring and summer of each year and worked on the house with Bill. Progress was slow because Ann continued work with the Rock Island and Bill worked part time on the house and part time at other jobs. Joost helped when he was home.

In May, 1961, Joost joined the US Navy. He worked on the house when home on leave. The house was finally finished in 1965 but proved difficult to sell even though it was well built. Helen and her husband John eventually bought the house.

In the spring of 1963, Joost was a petty officer serving on the USS Albany, an early guided missile cruiser of the Navy. That spring, a "Dependent's Cruise" was held for the families of crew members. Joost proudly invited the family. Bill, Ann, Bill Junior and youngest brother John traveled to Norfolk, Virginia to go to sea on the warship. They were duly impressed and thirteen old Johnny never forgot his excitement.

In the early spring of 1964, Ann's mother Lena was in a hospital in Enkhuizen. Doctors expected her to pass away soon. Ann wanted to come to say goodbye, which she soon did. Ann also contacted Joost, who was on the USS Albany in the Mediterranean Sea. Ann flew from Chicago to Amsterdam and a few days later, Joost left his ship in Naples. Ann and brother in law Simon Sluis were waiting at the Amsterdam Schiphol Airport for Joost's airplane when the airport announced that the Alitalia plane from Rome had crashed in the Alps. The two were waiting for a flight manifest to verify that Joost was indeed among the dead, when Joost appeared. It turned out that Joost had been waiting at the boarding gate in the Rome airport when an Alitalia stewardess informed him that he had to go to a different airplane. No reason was given. Another stewardess escorted Joost to the boarding gate of a different airline and the ticket was changed. Everyone was killed on the first airplane when it crashed in the Alps. No reason was ever discovered for the change. Joost and Ann spent a week in Enkhuizen saying goodbye to "Oma" Kuiper and becoming reacquainted with the families.

Bill and Ann celebrated their twenty fifth wedding anniversary in 1964. Ann was thrilled with her gift of a piano from her Bill and unpacked the sheet music from Beethoven, Brahms, Chopin and other masters that she had carefully carried to America. The violins were still in the attic and would not be played again. Ann had always done finger exercises to keep her hands nimble and now started playing again. Piano music returned to the house.

The Sluis family was now doing well. Joost was in the Navy, and father Bill was very proud of the fact. Helen was happily married. Bill was a college student and Ben was a new high school graduate. Little John was fourteen years old, a student at Lincoln Way and on the football team. Ann continued her advancement at the Rock Island. Bill drank a little too much wine but still worked to help support the family. There was now considerable talk about building a new house to replace the hand built one that had given the family so many hard years.

In 1968 the Sluis Brothers Seed Company in Enkhuizen, The Netherlands celebrated its centennial. The Queen knighted the director, Bill's brother Simon Sluis, and gave the company the designation Royal Sluis, which was accepted proudly as the new company name. A big celebration for all the current and past employees brought Bill and Ann from America to Enkhuizen. At the celebration banquet, Bill was honored at the head table as a former director and was presented with a custom painted plate in Delft Blue that showed a stagecoach traveling to Mokena. This valuable plate may be the only plate ever custom made by the Royal Delft Blue factory that shows a stagecoach and it was proudly displayed in the Sluis home back in Mokena.

The new house was started after a lot of discussion about its nature. The original plan was that it might be a duplex so as to provide income to Bill and Ann. After several years of discussion, a plan was selected. This time, a contractor was called in to build the basement and shell for the house, although Bill and the family did interior work such as wiring, and plumbing. A contractor was called in to do the interior drywall work so that the house was completed in a reasonable time. The old house was sold. Bill and Ann moved into their new house, next door to daughter Helen, in 1970. The piano occupied a place of honor in the house.

A problem with the new house was the stairway to the second

floor. Bill and Ann had brought their original "Bauhaus" bedroom set to America and treasured it even though the blond finish was becoming a little yellow with age. Bill had rewired the indirect lighting for U.S. lamp sockets. The headboard for the bed was about eleven feet long and could not be brought upstairs when the house was finished. After discussions that included redesigning the house, Bill decided that the house would have to be built around the headboard. This was done, and the headboard went into the house while it was being framed. It was carefully wrapped. The carpenters had to work around it and move it regularly. The large matching wardrobe with its built in vanity mirror would be disassembled and installed later since it and the night stands could go up the stairs.

"Bill and Ann's new house"

Ann was now "Oma" to Helen's children next door, to the rest of her growing list of grandchildren, and to the neighborhood. Life revolved around grandchildren, work and some community activities in Mokena. Ann was an early member of the Mokena Women's Club and Bill was in the Lions Club. Ann was, in the meantime promoted to Chief Timekeeper of the Rock Island Railroad; she was in charge of the payroll for the entire company.

In August 1976, at the age of 61, Ann had a serious heart attack or seizure while in Chicago. She was rushed to a hospital where her heart was defibrillated twice before it started to beat regularly again. Ann's working life was now over. She did not have enough time with the railroad for a full pension but did receive a smaller benefit. Medicine stabilized her condition.

Helen's husband John worked at the Argonne National Laboratory and he was able to help both his wife and Bill get work there. Bill ended up working in the library where his knowledge of languages served him well. Ann stayed home and had time for her grand children.

Bill retired at the age of 62 in 1977. Bill and Ann then bought a succession of travel trailers and made winter trips to Florida – trips they very much liked. Life was good and included several cruises, a couple of trips back to The Netherlands and a trip to Hawaii. On his last trip to Europe, Bill made a special visit to Saint Remy-De-Provence in southern France to visit his old friend Retou who was in a nursing home and in poor health. Bill's brother Simon helped make the arrangements for their farewell.

"Bill and Ann in retirement"

Toward the end of his life, Bill liked to sit in the travel trailer and smoke cigarettes while drinking wine. Ann made sure that he ate good food and kept as healthy as possible. His final victory was in 1983. Bill and Ann made an unusual fall 1982 visit to Joost and his family in Norfolk, Virginia. Joost was suspicious of the timing and noticed that Bill spent an unusual amount of time with the Norfolk grand children, especially with Joost's daughter Michelle who spent a lot of time listening to her grandfather in his trailer. Within a year, much loved and respected by all, Bill passed from this world. His body was buried in St. John's Cemetery in Mokena, less than 25 miles from the house in which he was born at 7043 South Sangamon Street in Chicago.

Bill's wry sense of humor followed him even after death. When the funeral was over, the family went to the "Cow Palace", a hall in Mokena, for a luncheon. While they were there, the Lutheran minister came to Joost with the horrible news that Bill had been returned to the funeral home in the back of a van because his casket did not fit into the burial vault. The Sluis family enjoyed this bit of news immensely since it squared fully with Bill's reputation that nothing he built would fit on the first try. It developed that the funeral home had obtained an oversized casket for Bill's large body but had forgotten to replace the burial vault with a larger one.

EPILOGUE

Renie

When Bill died in 1983, Ann was sixty eight years old. She was still an attractive woman since she had been careful all her life to maintain her figure and appearance. The men who had been neighbors both across the street from the old house and directly behind the house – one of whom had provided water in 1951 and the other electricity – both came calling as widowers to see if Ann might be interested in marrying them. Ireneus Jasinski (Renie), who had built his own house across the street had been a widower for about six years and became caller number three. Renie had retired a few years before from U.S. Steel.

Renie had been a close neighbor since 1952 and his family and the Sluis family had gone through a lot of life together. He was born in Chicago in 1912, like Bill had been in 1915, but his father had moved back to his native Poland when Renie was young. He returned to the United States as a teenager in the late 1930's because his friends advised him to get out of Poland because war was expected with Germany. Renie had graduated from a high school in Poland, which was unusual then. His high school class had 26 boys. He found out much later that 22 of his classmates had been officers in the Polish Army who were captured by the Russians and were later shot in the massacre in the Katyn Forest of March, 1940. Renie found that a surviving classmate lived in New York and communicated with him regularly.

Renie's first job in America was as an orderly in a hospital. He went to night school to learn English. The hospital was good to him since he also met his first wife Adeline there.

In 1944 Renie enlisted in the U.S. Navy to serve in World War II. He served in the air crew on several types of reconnaissance planes until he was demobilized from the service in 1946. He was proud of the fact that he was in the crew of the first airplane ever sent into a hurricane to measure wind speeds. After his Navy service he went to college at night on the G.I. Bill and earned a degree in metallurgy.

When Renie and Adeline moved to Mokena, he worked at the South Works of the United States Steel Corporation, testing metals. He and Adeline built their house in much the same way that Ann and Bill did. Their three children played with and fought with the Sluis kids as they grew up. Adeline worked in the flower business of Marge Bernardin for many years. Adeline died young at age 56 from cancer and Renie became a bachelor in Mokena who was in demand among the older ladies.

It happened that Ann and Renie were together at a dinner table with the Bishop of Joliet, Joseph Imesch. After a few glasses of wine all around, Renie turned to the Bishop and asked "If I ask this woman to marry me, will you do the ceremony"? The Bishop replied that he would be happy to since he had not married anyone in a long time. Ann then turned to the Bishop and explained that she was not Catholic. The Bishop allowed that he could fix that also. It happened, then, that a woman who came to Mokena from a small Netherlands city because of the fortunes of war married a second man who was born in Chicago and raised in Europe like her first husband had been. The Bishop married them in August, 1984 in the old "Pioneer" church the St Mary Parish in Mokena had outgrown years before. Ann was made Catholic at the same time. Joost retired from the Navy in time for the ceremony and gave the bride away. No novelist could have dreamed of it.

"Ann and Renie"

Ann was now Polish. Her official name became Ann May Sluis Jasinski because she had adopted the name Ann May when she was naturalized as an American Citizen. She had picked her middle name because she liked it and thought that having a middle name made hers more American. The Jasinski kids and the Sluis kids now had to be nicer to each other since they were now half brothers and sisters.

Renie and Ann lived in the "new" house that Bill and Ann had built. They were happy together and Ann was as supportive and loyal to Renie as she had been to Bill. Renie's former house was lent to his daughter Christine who was divorced and had two young children. Renie's son Tom lived about twenty miles away with his family while his other daughter Susan lived in Connecticut.

After a few years together in the large house in Sunny Acres, Ann and Renie decided that they should move to a smaller senior citizens apartment. They asked to be placed on a waiting list for a small community owned apartment and were able to move in after a short wait. They now lived in Senior Housing at Autumn Valley. The original coffee table, now worn with age, from Ann's wedding house in Enkhuizen still occupied the center of her living room.

Renie and Ann traveled to Europe together in 1987. Their first stop was in Krakow, Poland where Ann met Renie's sister and learned some Polish words. After visiting Warsaw and other relatives, the two went to The Netherlands where Renie met the Kuiper and Sluis families. Ann was popular in Poland. Renie was well liked by the Dutch relatives. It was a wonderful trip. They made several cruises together, the last with Joost and his wife Helen in 1992. There was also another trip to Poland and Holland. Both were slowing down.

When they married, each thought that the marriage would not last very long because they were already old. They agreed that each year should count as five. Their tenth wedding anniversary in 1995 was a big party for the entire Sluis-Jasinski family. Ann and Renie told everyone that they had not expected to live this long. Bishop Imesch and Simon Sluis' wife Ellie were at the head table. They renewed their wedding vows in church. It was officially the fiftieth anniversary!

Joost organized a trip to The Netherlands in 1998 to celebrate the fiftieth anniversary of coming to America. A group was organized that consisted of Joost and his wife Helen, Bill and his wife Carole, John and his wife Terry and Ann with Helen's oldest daughter Jackie. Ann was weak and in a wheelchair but anxious to go. Renie stayed home. Joost and Bill with their wives left first and took a bus tour through The Netherlands. Joost had been there several times but Bill had never been back to his birth place. John was born in Chicago so everything was new to him. After the tour group had traveled around Holland for five days, John and Terry came with Ann and Jackie. Simon Sluis met Ann with her entourage and took them to his house in Alkmaar so that Ann could rest. Joost had arranged to leave the bus tour before it ended by stepping off the bus in Delft.

In Delft, Joost and Bill, with their wives, met up with their cousin Jacob Sluis, Simon's oldest son who Joost had known for many years. The group went to the Delft railroad station and met John and his wife Terry when they arrived on a train. John and Terry loved the train trip from Alkmaar that Simon arranged for them. The group walked through Delft and saw the house where the Sluis family had lived during the war. Simon had contacted the owners of the house who graciously welcomed everyone inside. Joost was able to tell them something of the history of the house. The entire group then went to Enkhuizen in Jacob's mini bus.

In Enkhuizen they stayed at Die Port Van Cleve for several days. Simon brought Ann and Jackie from Alkmaar. Ann was put to bed to rest when she arrived. A few hours later, Jackie found Ann crying with happiness because she was listening to the bells of her childhood – the iron bells in the cupola of the Drommedaris and the carillon in the tower of the Zuider Kerk. Die Port Van Cleve and the Drommedaris are both near the eastern entrance of the old inner harbor while Ann's childhood home faces them both on the western end. Simon had arranged a family reception in the hall of Ann's wedding reception. Many family members came.

"Ann sitting on the bench of her childhood home after fifty years in America"

The group spent several days in Enkhuizen. The visiting couples were fascinated with the city and enjoyed meeting some of their cousins for the first time. Simon had made arrangements for the group to tour the ancient city hall and meet the mayor. The trip was an astounding success for all.

When 2000 came, life for Renie and Ann was becoming difficult. Neither of them could see very much any more and walking was getting harder. Ann had both of her hips replaced at age 77 because of arthritis but still had bad knees. Renie would go on walks by himself. He also spent a lot of time on his computer working on the mathematical theories and writing that were his hobbies. Ann still insisted on preparing meals although all the children were afraid of fire or injury at the Jasinski house. John's wife Terry started preparing ready made frozen meals. Joost's wife Helen placed Dr Scholls bunion pads on two of the microwave buttons so that Ann would know which buttons to push for warming things up. The Sluis children that lived nearby visited often to check up. Ann and Renie depended on each other and kept each other going.

Renie dreamed of living until the new millennium. He was thrilled to reach it and died on September 22, 2001. Ann and Renie had been married for seventeen years! Renie was cremated and his Jasinski children secretly scattered his ashes on the lawn of the house he built in Sunny Acres. His official burial place is next to his first wife Adeline in St Mary Cemetery in Mokena.

Ann bravely went on. She could no longer live alone. Joost and Helen lived in a large house and converted their living room to a temporary apartment for Ann, but the arrangement was too difficult and was abandoned after about five months. In 2002 she moved to Holy Family Villa, a Catholic nursing home ten miles North of Mokena. There she was loved by the staff as much as she had been by friends and family all her life. Her strength and positive outlook were an inspiration to all who met her. Ann was proud to have outlived everyone she knew. She triumphantly departed a few days before her 92nd birthday and is buried with her Willem in St John's Cemetery, Mokena.

"Ann's 88th birthday, with all her children"

The Children

Joost

Joost was a newspaper boy in his early teens and worked part time in a farm equipment repair shop, "Swanberg Farm and Auto Service" from the age of 15.

When he graduated from high school in the spring of 1958, he had won an Illinois State Scholarship to college. The scholarship paid full tuition of $600 per year and he had been accepted at the prestigious Illinois Institute of Technology as an architecture student. While Bill and Ann were in The Netherlands that summer, a letter came from the state that the scholarship had been revoked because no birth certificate was submitted. Joost did not have a birth certificate because all such papers were taken to Germany in during the war. When Bill and Ann called home to check up on the family, Joost reported the problem. Bill obtained a "Report of Birth" from the American Embassy in Amsterdam for Joost but both his passport and "Report of Birth" from the US State Department were rejected as acceptable proof. The scholarship was gone. The family did not have money for college.

Ann was highly respected at the Rock Island Railroad and had been promoted several times. She arranged for Joost to work at the railroad as a clerk.

Joost saved as much as he could from his railroad job and applied to the Massachusetts Institute of Technology, where he was accepted for the fall 1959 term.

In the fall of 1959, Joost traveled to Boston and enrolled at M.I.T. He was completely unprepared for life alone without the family. Joost could not adapt to the social pressures of living with strangers. He came home at Christmas and did not go back.

In the fall of 1960, Joost attended the University of Illinois but the result was like the year before.

Joost joined the U. S. Navy in May 1961. Because of his extremely high aptitude scores, the Navy placed him in the new field of guided missiles. It took several years for him to be granted the necessary security clearances because investigation in The Netherlands was required. His parents were very proud of the fact that their eldest son, who had barely survived World War II very frail and in leg braces, had become a strong man with strong legs. Bill was proud of the fact that his son was in the military carrying on the tradition of brother Joost. Whenever he was on leave, Joost would work on the house that his dad was slowly building.

Helen Sheridan had been a friend since she met Joost at Lincoln Way High School in 1956. The two were married in Mokena in 1967. Duty in the Navy brought them to Seattle, Washington; San Diego, Long Beach and Vallejo, California; Kiel, Germany and Norfolk, Virginia. Their four children were born in California, Germany and Virginia. The children were raised primarily in Norfolk where Joost and Helen bought a house. Joost retired from the Navy in 1984 as a Master Chief.

After the Navy, Joost and Helen built a home in Mokena. Joost worked as a Field Engineer in the controls business and Helen eventually worked in the County Auditors Office. Both retired in 2002.

Helen

Bill and Ann's daughter Helen was an attractive girl with many friends. When she graduated in 1959, she went to work in downtown Chicago. Her blue 1960 Chevrolet Bel Air was the pride of her young life. She used to drive the Bel Air to the Mokena train station in order to commute to work in Chicago. One day the car was missing when she came home on the train. The police were called and it turned out that brother Ben had borrowed the keys to have a duplicate made. Ben was caught and Helen was mad. The car did not leave the station without permission after that.

Helen married John Weber and had four children. John was a technician at the Argonne National Laboratory. The house that Bill started building in 1960 was completed in 1965. The house proved difficult to sell even though it was in a popular style and well built. Helen and her husband John bought the house so that Helen's four children grew up living next door to Ann "Oma" Sluis to the satisfaction of all. "Oma" spent many afternoons with the grandchildren from next door.

John Weber was a friendly man who helped Bill finish work in the basement of the house. John was popular in Mokena where he was active in the Lions Club. Helen and John's house was a social magnet for the family and many happy days were spent there in family parties and picnics.

Helen went to work when her children were still relatively small. Having "Oma" Ann and "Opa" Bill next door proved to be a wonderful thing although a neighbor was officially in charge of the children. Helen had a very successful career at Argonne where she eventually became a senior executive secretary. She divorced John after many years and later remarried with Herbert Gramse. Helen and Herb moved to Forsyth, Missouri after retirement.

William

Bill Jr. was of fairly small build but outgoing and popular in school. He was interested in sports and became the manager of several sports teams at Lincoln Way High School. He was also interested in writing and started writing reports of basketball and football games for the "Joliet Herald". His writing career as a manager set the pattern for his life. Bill won a McCormick scholarship to the prestigious Medill School of Journalism at Northwestern University and graduated after five years with a Master's Degree.

After graduation, the draft placed him in the U.S. Army for a trip to Vietnam. The army offered Bill a commission because of his college degree but he refused on the grounds that he would have to spend more than two years in the army. Bill went to Vietnam and was assigned as a reporter for the 25th Infantry Division. He traveled between artillery bases and other facilities to write about the troops. His fellow draftees adored the fact that he had refused the commission.

In 1966 Bill was reporting on troop activities at a Michelin Rubber Company plantation near the Cambodian border when North Vietnamese and Viet Cong troops overran the plantation. Bill and several other men hid, unarmed, on the second floor of a house. Father Bill and Ann received a terrible shock with news that Bill was missing. A few days later, the 25th Division was able to retake the plantation and found Bill and his friends still alive in the upstairs room. Bill was able to call home to report that he was O.K. Bill was a brave soldier who was awarded the Bronze Star.

In 1969, Bill married Carole Mahan. Bill had worked at various jobs after the Army but now was a newspaper reporter for the Chicago Tribune. Bill and Carole lived in several Chicago suburbs until they bought a home and settled in Mokena. They had two children.

In 1981 while working as a reporter, Bill saw a man lurching toward his car while driving on the lower level of Wacker Drive in Chicago. Lower Wacker Drive was the basement access to numerous tall buildings and home to vagrants who lived in cardboard boxes above exhaust ducts from the downtown skyscrapers of the city. Ignoring the danger, Bill stopped and found that the man was a taxi driver who had been stabbed by a thief who stole his taxi. He took the stabbed man to the hospital, saved his life by doing so, and was publicly recognized as a hero by the Chicago Police.

Bill ultimately served on the editorial staff of the Tribune where he spent his entire professional career. Bill retired in 2008 after forty years with the newspaper.

Bernard

After graduation from Lincoln Way High School in 1964, Ben bought a beautiful Mercury Monterrey convertible. It was a gorgeous car and the envy of the neighborhood. The girls loved riding in it. Ben started work at a few places but remained dissatisfied and ended up joining the U.S. Marines. He served honorably in Viet Nam where he was a radio operator. On leaving the Marines, he came home for a short while and established himself with a job for an import export company.

Ben earned a college degree by working at various jobs and going to school. He achieved a Bachelors Degree from Governors State University and became a professional auditor. Ben advanced his career as an auditor for the State of California and ended it with a very successful career as a tax auditor for the State of Florida. He lived in Chicago and audited the books of companies that earned part of their income in Florida.

Ben was married several times and had no children. His last wife Linda Koziol was a cousin of Renie Jasinski's children and had played with them in Mokena when young. Linda had two children who brought Ben and Linda three grand children. Ben was a happy "Opa" when he retired in 2008.

John

John was born in Chicago and grew up in Mokena. He was very young when his parents were going through the trauma of living in an incomplete house and was not much affected by it.

John was popular in school and played on the Lincoln Way football team. On graduation from high school, he went to Valparaiso University in Indiana with a scholarship to study engineering. He graduated with a degree in Mechanical Engineering. While going to the University, he also worked for the Elgin, Joliet and Eastern Railroad in Joliet, Illinois. He worked the evening shift in the railroad yard and eventually became a foreman. His high speed travels back and forth between school and job with his beloved Pontiac GTO car were legend.

John married an attractive girl he had met at a party but the marriage was short lived. John and his wife Connie had a son, John Paul. Connie left after a short marriage and John remained a bachelor until he met Terry, his second wife.

John worked as a Controls Engineer for a company named Johnson Controls for about seven years and was then hired by Iowa State University. John worked very happily for Iowa State designing and installing major control systems until he was hired by the Wheaton Schools to be their Director of Buildings. This was his dream job, and he excelled in it. He and Terry had lived in Mokena, Bondurant, Iowa and Wheaton. Terry's daughter Lisa, from a first marriage, loved John as much as Terry.

John unexpectedly died of a massive heart attack at the young age of 53. His mother Ann was living in Holy Family Villa and had celebrated her birthday the day before John's death. Ann was not very alert anymore. When the wake was held in Wheaton, Ann came, in her wheel chair, and rallied to give strength to everyone there. John is buried near his father and mother in St John's Cemetery, Mokena.

Enkhuizen

After World War II, Enkhuizen entered the twentieth century. The city has been designated a "museum city" to preserve its heritage from the Golden Age. Because of the city's designation, house facades in Enkhuizen are maintained in their sixteenth century appearance while the interiors are often modernized. Old West Frisian buildings from many locales have been dismantled and rebuilt outside the old city walls of the Wierdyk that was once a place for ship building. A large collection of historic buildings has been reconstructed there to complement the city with its historic legacy. The "Zuider Zee Museum" has historically correct shops and demonstrations of ancient skills. Relocated stores have clerks in traditional costume and sell numerous authentic items. The East India Company warehouses that used to stand on the harbor near Ann's childhood home have been dismantled and moved to the Zuider Zee Museum outside the city. It is a major learning center and tourist attraction.

The city is successful again as a choice destination for the yachts of northern Europe. The Drommedaris and many other historic places in the city have become restaurants and bars while keeping their sixteenth century façade. On summer weekends the city fills up with partying visitors who often come on their yachts. The fishing industry is no longer needed. Many remaining old Zuider Zee boats have been brought to Enkhuizen where several large companies offer week long sailing charters and day trips on classic restored boats.

Mokena

Mokena grew rapidly after the 1950's. Most of the businesses on Front Street closed as the automobile gave people more and more freedom to select shopping locales. The village grew to a population of about eighteen thousand by the year 2,000 because growth of the City of Chicago turned it into a suburb. The little Catholic parish on the outside of the town ended up building a new large church because a large percentage of new arrivals in the town were Roman Catholic. The little village school that the Sluis children attended became the Village Hall after it was outgrown. Lincoln Way High school had about 400 students when it opened in 1954 but grew to several schools with five thousand students. When the millennium came, Mokena and other nearby towns were pleasant suburbs that only vaguely remembered their farming heritage.